Natural Recipes for the Good Life

Natural Recipes for the Good Life

Using Wholesome Ingredients for Better Health

— ◄►—

Hedi Levine

≣**People's Medical Society**®

Allentown, PA

The People's Medical Society is a nonprofit consumer health organization dedicated to the principles of better, more responsive and less expensive medical care. Organized in 1983, the People's Medical Society puts previously unavailable medical information into the hands of consumers so that they can make informed decisions about their own health care.

Membership in the People's Medical Society is $20 a year and includes a subscription to the *People's Medical Society Newsletter.* For information, write to the People's Medical Society, 462 Walnut Street, Allentown, PA 18102, or call 610-770-1670.

This and other People's Medical Society publications are available for quantity purchase at discount. Contact the People's Medical Society for details.

Library of Congress Cataloging-in-Publication Data

Levine, Hedi.
    Natural recipes for the good life : using wholesome ingredients for better health / Hedi Levine.
        p.   cm.
    Includes index.
    ISBN 1-882606-74-4 (pbk.)
    1. Cookery (Natural foods)   2. Natural foods.   I. Natural health.
II. Title.
TX741.L45   1997
641.5'63–dc21
                                                        96-50005
                                                          CIP

Produced by Tripart, Ltd.
118 East 25th Street
New York, NY 10010

Creative Director: Tony Meisel
Editorial Director: Hedi Levine
Editor: Sarah May Clarkson
Composition: Diane Specioso

PhotoDisc Image © 1997 PhotoDisc, Inc. for front cover photograph.

Manufactured in the United States of America

ISBN 1-882606-74-4

CONTENTS

Introduction • 7

Breakfast • 9

Breads & Muffins • 21

Starters & Snacks • 45

Soups • 55

Salads • 75

Rice & Grains • 95

Beans & Legumes • 109

Pasta & Noodles • 121

Main Courses • 141

Vegetables • 167

Condiments • 187

Desserts • 199

Glossary • 217

Index • 221

INTRODUCTION

When we shop for natural foods, our choices are driven by a desire to feel good now and to remain healthy longer; to help prevent diseases and unhealthy conditions–like heart disease, a variety of cancers, obesity and high blood pressure–that often relate directly to diet; and to protect the earth with sustainable farming practices.

These goals are mirrored by food manufacturers who grow and process the natural foods we buy. Their priorities are reflected in products that are processed without synthetic additives, artificial colors, flavors, sweeteners and hydrogenated or solvent-extracted oils; and in foods grown without using pesticides, herbicides and fungicides in soil that has been free of chemicals for at least three years. These products can be labeled *certified organic* if the farms are evaluated by an outside organization.

Healthy eating means different things to different people. Always has. Is there a politically correct way to eat? Would everyone agree what it is? Is there a consensus about anything concerning our diets and a diet for a healthy planet? Certain concepts stand out like bullets: low fat (anywhere from 30 percent of calories consumed to the more stringent 20 percent); low sodium (less than 2,400 milligrams [mg] daily); complex carbohydrates; and high fiber. Experts agree that diets designed to cure health ills or to prevent them converge on a common principle: Eat a wide variety of unprocessed high-carbohydrate foods in moderate amounts.

The key to good nutrition is balance and moderation. Don't get carried away by fad diets. Don't eat until you feel like bursting. Balance recipes that are higher in fat and sodium with those that are lower. Eat lots of fruits and vegetables, cut down on meat, eat more fish and complex carbohydrates.

In other words, eat your starch, eat your vegetables and eat a lot of different kinds.

To maintain a dietary ideal of variety and moderation does not require that you eliminate any one food group from your diet. Since animal foods are higher in fat, especially saturated fats, it is important to balance their place in your diet with ample plant sources of protein as well. But in any case, look for meat, chicken and fish that have been healthfully raised.

Some individuals, some families, perhaps some populations are at a higher risk for high blood pressure caused by high-sodium diets. But a low-sodium diet hurts no one. About 1,000 mg a day are recommended. Processed foods contain lots of secret salt. Read labels. And when cooking, minimize salt by heightening flavors in other ways. Fresh herbs are a wonderful antidote to the tendency to salt food beyond what's necessary for flavor or recommended for health.

Regardless of who grows and processes your food, you are responsible for putting together meals that are a balance of the starches, vegetables and protein you and your family need to maintain health. The recipes collected in *Natural Recipes for the Good Life* have not been adapted to meet any particular dietary standard. We have developed and tested them so that you can easily assemble healthful meals from the ingredients you have easy access to in the stores. But when you cook from the recipes in this book–or any cookbook, for that matter—always apply your dietary needs to the recipe and the meal.

For example, soy sauce is sodium. You can reduce a recipe's sodium content by cutting the salt or soy sauce in half or substituting low-sodium soy sauce. Cut fat calories by using minimal oil and sautéing in nonstick skillets. Substitute low-fat or nonfat soy milk for regular soy milk or whole dairy milk. Above all, enjoy the universe of foods available to you.

In the summer months be grateful for the local produce you can buy in your farmer's market; in the fall be grateful for the potatoes, squash and chard that you can get there. In the dead of winter be grateful for the produce available in your natural foods store. When you shop there you can see your priorities reflected on the shelves. And when you take the food home and prepare it, you will see your own best intentions fulfilled.

Notes: To calculate the percentage of calories from fat in any recipe, multiply the number of grams of fat times nine and divide by the total number of calories.

When a recipe calls for alcoholic ingredients, remember that most of the alcohol will burn off in cooking, leaving just the flavor. If you would prefer not to use alcohol, an equal amount of stock, broth or nonalcoholic wine may be used.

Some of the ingredients used in these recipes may be unfamiliar to you. Don't let this keep you from trying them. However, be forewarned that certain chile peppers–habañero, Scotch bonnet, Szechuan and birds-eye–are positively incendiary. Use with caution!

The recipes contained in this book have been tested and carefully edited by the publisher. The publisher cannot be held responsible for any ill effects caused by errors in the recipes or by spoiled ingredients, unsanitary conditions, incorrect preparation procedures or any other cause.

Breakfast

GLUTEN-FREE PANCAKES

1 cup (240 ml) rice or millet flour
½ cup (120 ml) soy flour
½ cup (120 ml) cornmeal
1 tbsp (15 ml) non-alum baking powder
¼ tsp (1 ml) sea salt, optional
1 egg, beaten
1½ cups (355 ml) water
2 tbsp (30 ml) unrefined vegetable oil

Combine all dry ingredients. Stir together all liquids; add to dry ingredients. Bake on preheated 350-375°F (180-190°C) griddle. Turn only once. Yields 12 pancakes.

Approximate nutritional analysis per 3-pancake serving:
Calories 332, Protein 9 g, Carbohydrates 50 g, Fat 11 g, Cholesterol 47 mg, Sodium 382 mg

SOUR CREAM-APPLE PANCAKES

¾ cup (180 ml) whole wheat flour
1 tsp (5 ml) non-alum baking powder
½ tsp (3 ml) sea salt, optional
¼ tsp (1 ml) cinnamon
1 tbsp (15 ml) honey
1 medium apple, grated
1 egg, beaten, or egg replacer
1 tsp (5 ml) pure vanilla
½ cup (120 ml) sour cream
1 cup (240 ml) water or buttermilk

In large bowl combine dry ingredients. Combine remaining ingredients, mixing well; add to dry ingredients and stir until just blended. Cook on preheated 350°F (180°C) griddle for 3-5 minutes, turning only once. Serve hot. Yields 12 pancakes.

Approximate nutritional analysis per 3-pancake serving:
Calories 194, Protein 5 g, Carbohydrates 28 g, Fat 8 g, Cholesterol 60 mg, Sodium 153 mg

POTATO PANCAKES

2 cups (480 ml) potato flakes
¼ cup (60 ml) gluten-free pancake mix
2½ cups (590 ml) water
1 small onion, diced
1 egg, beaten
½ tsp (3 ml) onion powder, garlic powder or lemon pepper, optional

Mix first two ingredients. Stir in water and onion. Stir in egg. For spicier cakes add onion or garlic powder or lemon pepper to dry mixture. Salt and pepper to taste. Let stand 1-2 minutes. Bake on well-oiled, preheated 350-375°F (180-190°C) griddle until golden brown. Turn once. Serves 4.

Approximate nutritional analysis per serving:
Calories 128, Protein 4 g, Carbohydrates 25 g, Fat 2 g, Cholesterol 47 mg, Sodium 84 mg

WHOLE GRAIN WAFFLES

⅔ cup (160 ml) whole wheat flour
⅔ cup (160 ml) brown rice flour
⅔ cup (160 ml) low-fat soy flour
1 tsp (5 ml) baking soda
1 tsp (5 ml) baking powder
½ tsp (3 ml) salt
2 tbsp (30 ml) wheat germ
1½ cups (355 ml) skim milk
1 cup (240 ml) nonfat plain yogurt
3 tbsp (45 ml) butter, melted
3 eggs, separated

Whisk together the flours, baking soda, baking powder, salt and wheat germ in a large bowl. In a smaller bowl mix together the milk, yogurt, cooled butter and egg yolks. Add the milk mixture to the dry ingredients and stir until everything is thoroughly blended.

In a separate bowl whip the egg whites until stiff peaks form. Fold the egg whites into the batter. Cook on a hot, oiled waffle iron. Yields 10 waffles.

Approximate nutritional analysis per waffle:
Calories 168, Protein 9 g, Carbohydrates 21 g, Fat 2 g, Cholesterol 67 mg, Sodium 373 mg

WOW! WAFFLES

3 eggs, separated
2¼ cups (540 ml) nonfat plain yogurt
2 tbsp (30 ml) nonfat dry milk
½ tsp (3 ml) baking soda
1 tbsp (15 ml) honey
⅓ cup (80 ml) quick-cooking oats
⅓ cup (80 ml) cornmeal
⅓ cup (80 ml) margarine or butter, melted
1 cup (240 ml) unbleached all-purpose flour
1 tbsp (15 ml) baking powder
pinch salt, optional
1-2 tbsp (15-30 ml) milk, optional

Combine the egg yolks, yogurt, dry milk, baking soda and honey in a large bowl. Beat with a wire whisk. Stir in the oats and cornmeal, then add the margarine and stir again. Sift in the flour, baking powder and salt. Beat well, then cover the bowl and let the mixture sit for 15 minutes. Beat the egg whites until stiff, then fold them into the mixture. If the batter is too thick, add 1-2 tbsp milk.

Preheat a waffle iron to the high setting, oil it and cook the batter. Serve the waffles on warm plates. Yields 8 waffles.

As accompaniments, you might offer warm maple syrup; fresh, sliced fruit or berries; and yogurt.

To freeze the waffles, cool them on a rack, then place the rack of waffles in the freezer. Store the frozen waffles in tightly sealed plastic bags. To reheat, pop them in the toaster.

Approximate nutritional analysis per waffle:
Calories 234, Protein 9 g, Carbohydrates 27 g, Fat 10 g, Cholesterol 92 mg, Sodium 497 mg

WAFFLES-N-FRUIT

1 cup (240 ml) soy milk
3 tbsp (45 ml) canola oil
2 eggs
2 tsp (10 ml) honey, optional
1½ cups (355 ml) flour
1 tbsp (15 ml) non-alum baking powder
½ tsp (3 ml) salt, optional
½ cup (120 ml) fruit, cut into small pieces

In medium bowl combine soy milk, oil, eggs and honey. Beat well with electric mixer.
   In separate bowl sift together flour, baking powder and salt. Add liquid ingredients to dry and beat well. Add more soy milk if necessary to obtain batter the consistency of heavy cream. (Thin batter makes tender waffles.) Add fruit to batter. Cook in preheated waffle iron. Yields 10 waffles.

Approximate nutritional analysis per waffle:
Calories 140, Protein 4 g, Carbohydrates 20 g, Fat 5 g, Cholesterol 35 mg, Sodium 140 mg

BARLEY-AMARANTH WAFFLES

¾ cup (180 ml) amaranth flour
1 cup (240 ml) barley flour
1 tbsp (15 ml) non-alum baking powder
¼ tsp (1 ml) sea salt, optional
1½ cups (355 ml) skim milk, soy milk or water
3 tbsp (45 ml) unrefined vegetable oil

Combine dry and liquid ingredients separately, then mix liquid ingredients into dry with hand mixer. Pour onto hot, nonstick griddle. Thin batter with additional water if needed.
May be used for pancakes also. Yields 4 waffles.

Approximate nutritional analysis per waffle:
Calories 423, Protein 14 g, Carbohydrates 63 g, Fat 14 g, Cholesterol 2 mg, Sodium 426 mg

CREAMY PEACH MELBA BREAKFAST BREAD

3 eggs
½ cup (120 ml) light cream or half-and-half
1 cup (240 ml) low-fat peach yogurt
1 cup (240 ml) low-fat raspberry yogurt
1 tsp (5 ml) vanilla
1 loaf Italian, French or challah bread, thickly sliced
1 tbsp (15 ml) oil
1 tbsp (15 ml) butter or margarine
fresh peaches or raspberries, for garnish
low-fat peach or raspberry yogurt, for garnish

Beat the eggs and combine with the cream, yogurts and vanilla. Mix well. Pour into one or two shallow rectangular pans. Place the bread in the egg mixture, cover and let stand overnight, turning once or twice during the standing period to make sure the mixture soaks through the slices.

The next morning, prepare a hot nonstick griddle or frying pan with a combination of vegetable oil and butter or margarine. Lightly brown each side of the bread slices, cooking slowly over low heat to firm the custard. Serve immediately with a garnish of fresh peach slices or raspberries and a dollop of peach or raspberry yogurt. Serves 5.

Approximate nutritional analysis per serving:
Calories 475, Protein 17 g, Carbohydrates 68 g, Fat 15 g, Cholesterol 131 mg, Sodium 684 mg

WILD RICE & DRIED FRUIT CEREAL

2 cups (480 ml) cooked wild rice
1¾ cups (415 ml) water
1 cup (240 ml) oats
⅔ cup (160 ml) raisins or chopped dried apricots, dates
    or other dried fruit
¼ tsp (1 ml) ground cinnamon
brown sugar or honey

In medium saucepan combine cooked rice with water, oats, fruit and cinnamon. Bring mixture to boiling; reduce heat. Cook, stirring frequently, about 5 minutes, or until oats are done. Serve as hot cereal with brown sugar or honey. Serves 4.

Approximate nutritional analysis per 1-cup serving:
Calories 244, Protein 7 g, Carbohydrates 53 g, Fat 2 g, Cholesterol 0 mg, Sodium 7 mg

WHEAT BERRY PORRIDGE

1 cup (240 ml) uncooked wheat berries
2 cups (480 ml) water
1 cup (240 ml) nonfat plain yogurt
¼ cup (60 ml) fresh lemon juice
1 unpeeled apple, cored and grated
2 bananas, sliced
2 peaches, peeled, pitted and sliced
1-2 cups (240-480 ml) grapes, halved
¼ tsp (1 ml) ground ginger
½ tsp (3 ml) ground cinnamon
pinch ground nutmeg

Cook the wheat berries in water over low heat for 4-6 hours or until the water is absorbed. (A crockpot is especially useful for this step.) Remove from heat and allow the berries to cool, then mix in the remaining ingredients and chill. Let stand for 30 minutes at room temperature before serving. Serves 4.

Approximate nutritional analysis per serving:
Calories 175, Protein 6 g, Carbohydrates 40 g, Fat .9 g, Cholesterol 1 mg, Sodium 48 mg

SWISS-STYLE OATS

3 cups (720 ml) water
1 cup (240 ml) chopped mixed dried fruit
1 tsp (5 ml) sea salt, optional
2 tbsp (30 ml) honey
1⅓ cups (320 ml) oat flakes (rolled oats)
2 tbsp (30 ml) wheat germ
¼ cup (60 ml) slivered almonds, toasted

Bring water to boil; stir in fruit, salt and honey. Bring to boil again. Add oats; stir; lower heat to simmer. Cover and simmer 15 minutes. Stir before serving. Sprinkle each serving with 1½ tsp wheat germ and 1 tbsp almonds. Serve with milk. Serves 4.

Approximate nutritional analysis per serving:
Calories 264, Protein 7 g, Carbohydrates 51 g, Fat 5 g, Cholesterol 0 mg, Sodium 9 mg

A BALANCED BREAKFAST

1 large unpeeled apple, cored and diced
¾ cup (180 ml) oat flakes (rolled oats)
¼ cup (60 ml) maple syrup
½ cup (120 ml) chopped walnuts
1 cup (240 ml) nonfat plain yogurt
2 tbsp (30 ml) wheat germ
ground cinnamon, optional
ground nutmeg, optional

Stir the apple, oats, maple syrup and walnuts into the yogurt. Sprinkle with wheat germ. Top with cinnamon and nutmeg. Serves 2.

Approximate nutritional analysis per serving:
Calories 543, Protein 21 g, Carbohydrates 74 g, Fat 7 g, Cholesterol 2 mg, Sodium 99 mg

SURPRISE BREAKFAST PUFFERS

4 tbsp (60 ml) orange marmalade
1 tsp (5 ml) grated orange rind
¼ tsp (1 ml) cinnamon
¼ tsp (1 ml) nutmeg
¼ cup (60 ml) butter
¼ cup (60 ml) honey
2 eggs
2 cups (480 ml) whole wheat flour
2 tsp (10 ml) non-alum baking powder
½ tsp (3 ml) sea salt, optional
1 cup (240 ml) buttermilk

Combine first four ingredients; set aside. In mixing bowl cream butter and honey; add eggs, one at a time until well blended. Gradually stir in next three ingredients; mix well. Slowly add buttermilk. Spoon 2 tbsp batter into oiled muffin cups; add 1 tsp orange filling and fill ⅔ full with batter. Bake in preheated 400°F (205°C) oven for 20-25 minutes. Yields 12.

Approximate nutritional analysis per puffer:
Calories 162, Protein 5 g, Carbohydrates 26 g, Fat 5 g, Cholesterol 46 mg, Sodium 128 mg

BULGUR WHEAT "SAUSAGE" PATTIES

2 cups (480 ml) cooked bulgur wheat or 1 cup (240 ml) raw
1 tbsp (15 ml) crushed basil leaves
1 egg
¾ tsp (4 ml) sage
¾ tsp (4 ml) poultry seasoning
¾ cup (180 ml) grated cheddar cheese, optional
¼ cup (60 ml) whole wheat flour
oil or nonstick spray

Mix the bulgur wheat, basil, egg, sage, poultry seasoning and cheese together. Salt to taste. Chill slightly. Form into patties and dip in whole wheat flour. Fry in a small amount of oil until lightly browned. These may be wrapped in individual packages and reheated. Cook like hamburger meat or add to casseroles in place of meat. Yields 8 medium patties or 30 sausage balls.

Variation: Form into cocktail-size balls and serve with sweet and sour sauce.

Approximate nutritional analysis per patty w/o cheese:
Calories 61, Protein 3 g, Carbohydrates 12 g, Fat .8 g, Cholesterol 0 mg, Sodium 9 mg

Approximate nutritional analysis per patty w/cheese:
Calories 103, Protein 5 g, Carbohydrates 12 g, Fat 4 g, Cholesterol 11 mg, Sodium 75 mg

Approximate nutritional analysis per sausage ball w/o cheese:
Calories 16, Protein .7 g, Carbohydrates 3 g, Fat .2 g, Cholesterol 0 mg, Sodium 2 mg

Approximate nutritional analysis per sausage ball w/cheese:
Calories 28, Protein 1 g, Carbohydrates 3 g, Fat 1 g, Cholesterol 3 mg, Sodium 20 mg

BREAKFAST HASH

1-2 tbsp (15-30 ml) olive oil
1 cup (240 ml) soy sausage, prepared and chopped
1 large potato, boiled, peeled and cut into small slices
1 large onion, chopped
1 clove garlic, diced or puréed
pinch black pepper
¼ tsp (1 ml) salt

Heat oil in skillet, add all ingredients, cover and sauté until crisp and brown; then turn over and sauté other side. Serves 8.

Approximate nutritional analysis per serving:
Calories 188, Protein 18 g, Carbohydrates 18 g, Fat 2 g, Cholesterol 0 mg, Sodium 218 mg

APPLE DUMPLINGS

2 cups (480 ml) flour
¼ tsp (1 ml) salt
3 tbsp (45 ml) sugar
1 tbsp (15 ml) baking powder
¾ cup (180 ml) unsalted butter
½ cup (120 ml) skim milk or buttermilk
3 apples, peeled, cored and quartered

Combine flour, salt, 2 tbsp sugar and baking powder and mix in cold butter with fingers. Add skim milk. Work into dough.

Roll out dough into 12 circles. Place one apple quarter in each piece of dough. Pinch dough closed. Sprinkle remaining sugar over dumplings. Place on greased cookie sheet and bake in pre-heated 350°F (180°C) oven for 35-40 minutes until golden brown. Yields 12 dumplings.

Approximate nutritional analysis per dumpling:
Calories 215, Protein 3 g, Carbohydrates 25 g, Fat 12 g, Cholesterol 31 mg, Sodium 135 mg

SOUTHWEST TOFU SCRAMBLER

1½ medium potatoes or 1 large potato
10½-oz pkg (315 g) light tofu, firm, crumbled
2 tsp (10 ml) margarine
2 dashes turmeric
¼ cup (60 ml) chopped green onion
¾ cup (180 ml) julienned red pepper
1 cup (240 ml) sliced mushrooms
3 tbsp (45 ml) picante sauce

Microwave potatoes for 5-6 minutes on high or use baked potatoes. Cool and slice thin. Add crumbled tofu to melted margarine in nonstick skillet. Add turmeric and cook on high for 5 minutes. Add vegetables and potato and cook 5 minutes or until vegetables are tender crisp. Stir in picante sauce and serve. Serves 2.

Approximate nutritional analysis per 1⅓-cup serving:
Calories 231, Protein 14 g, Carbohydrates 33 g, Fat 6 g, Cholesterol 0 mg, Sodium 354 mg

Breads & Muffins

HONEY WHEAT SODA BREAD

2 cups (480 ml) whole wheat flour
½ tsp (3 ml) salt
1 tsp (5 ml) baking soda
2 tbsp (30 ml) honey
1 cup (240 ml) buttermilk
1 egg, slightly beaten

In large mixing bowl combine flour, salt and baking soda. Make a well in the center. Add honey, buttermilk and egg. Stir just until moistened. Batter will be soft. Place in greased 1-quart casserole. Bake at 375°F (190°C) for 20-25 minutes. Cool completely before slicing. Serves 12.

Approximate nutritional analysis per serving:
Calories 92, Protein 4 g, Carbohydrates 19 g, Fat 1 g, Cholesterol 16 mg, Sodium 168 mg

SPICY BROWN BREAD

¾ cup (180 ml) blue cornmeal
¾ cup (180 ml) whole wheat pastry flour
2 tsp (10 ml) non-alum baking powder
¼ tsp (1 ml) sea salt, optional
2 tsp (10 ml) carob powder
½ tsp (3 ml) cinnamon
½ tsp (3 ml) ginger
½ tsp (3 ml) nutmeg
¾ cup (180 ml) milk or soy milk
½ cup (120 ml) unsulphured molasses
1 tsp (5 ml) lemon extract

Combine dry and liquid ingredients in separate bowls, then stir together until smooth. Batter seems thin, but it will thicken. Pour batter into oiled cupcake or loaf pan. Bake at 350°F (180°C) for 20 minutes or until knife test proves done. Yields 6 cupcakes or one 8-inch-square loaf.

Approximate nutritional analysis per serving:
Calories 197, Protein 5 g, Carbohydrates 44 g, Fat 1 g, Cholesterol 1 mg, Sodium 196 mg

CRANBERRY BREAD

2 cups (480 ml) whole wheat flour
1½ tsp (8 ml) non-alum baking powder
1 tsp (5 ml) sea salt, optional
¼ cup (60 ml) nonfat instant milk powder, optional
juice of 1 orange
2 tbsp (30 ml) unrefined safflower oil
hot water (140°F [60°C])
¾ cup (180 ml) raw honey
1 egg, beaten, or egg replacer
1 cup (240 ml) chopped walnuts
1 tbsp (15 ml) grated orange rind, optional
1 cup (240 ml) whole raw cranberries

Mix the flour, baking powder, salt and milk powder. Mix the orange juice and oil. Add enough hot water to bring liquid ingredients to ¾ cup (180 ml). Add the honey and egg to the liquid. Stir the liquid ingredients into the dry mixture. Add the nuts, orange rind and berries and fold together. Pour into an oiled loaf pan. Bake at 325°F (165°C) for 50 minutes to 1 hour. Cool on rack. Serve plain or lightly buttered. Yields 1 loaf.

Approximate nutritional analysis per slice:
Calories 341, Protein 9 g, Carbohydrates 52 g, Fat 13 g, Cholesterol 23 mg, Sodium 102 mg

CRANBERRY-OAT BREAD

¾ cup (180 ml) honey
⅓ cup (80 ml) vegetable oil
2 eggs
½ cup (120 ml) skim milk
2½ cups (590 ml) all-purpose flour
1 cup (240 ml) quick-cooking rolled oats
1 tsp (5 ml) baking soda
1 tsp (5 ml) baking powder
½ tsp (3 ml) salt
½ tsp (3 ml) ground cinnamon
2 cups (480 ml) fresh or frozen cranberries
1 cup (240 ml) chopped nuts

Combine honey, oil, eggs and milk in large bowl; mix well. Combine flour, oats, baking soda, baking powder, salt and cinnamon in medium bowl; mix well. Stir liquid ingredients into dry mixture. Fold in cranberries and nuts. Spoon into two 8½x4½x2½-inch greased and floured loaf pans.

Bake in preheated 350°F (180°C) oven for 40-45 minutes or until wooden toothpick inserted near center comes out clean.

Cool in pans on wire racks 15 minutes. Remove from pans; cool completely on wire racks. Yields 2 loaves.

Approximate nutritional analysis per slice:
Calories 256, Protein 7 g, Carbohydrates 36 g, Fat 10 g, Cholesterol 25 mg, Sodium 203 mg

BERRY BREAKFAST CAKE

1½ cups (355 ml) blue cornmeal
½ cup (120 ml) unbleached white flour
1 tbsp (15 ml) non-alum baking powder
2 egg whites
½ cup (120 ml) blueberry or boysenberry syrup
1 tbsp (15 ml) unrefined vegetable oil
1½ cups (355 ml) skim milk or soy milk
1 cup (240 ml) blueberries or boysenberries

Combine first three ingredients. Beat egg whites until fluffy. Beat together berry syrup, oil and milk, and gently fold in egg whites. Stir in dry ingredients, pour batter into oiled cake pan, sprinkle with berries and place on baking sheet. Bake at 425°F (220°C) for 30 minutes until golden. Serve hot with butter or your favorite syrup. Yields 1 loaf.

Approximate nutritional analysis per slice:
Calories 220, Protein 6 g, Carbohydrates 44 g, Fat 2 g, Cholesterol < 1 mg, Sodium 83 mg

BLUE CORN BREAD

1 cup (240 ml) blue cornmeal
½ cup (120 ml) barley flour or whole wheat flour
1½ tsp (8 ml) non-alum baking powder
¼ tsp (1 ml) sea salt, optional
1 tbsp (15 ml) honey or maple syrup
1 egg, beaten, or egg replacer
1 cup water or milk

Combine liquids and slowly add to combined dry ingredients. Oil bread or muffin pan. Bake at 425°F (220°C) for 15-20 minutes, until top and sides become golden brown. Yields one 8-inch loaf or 6 muffins.

Approximate nutritional analysis per muffin:
Calories 134, Protein 4 g, Carbohydrates 27 g, Fat 2 g, Cholesterol 31 mg, Sodium 139 mg

MAPLE SYRUP CORN BREAD

1 cup (240 ml) cornmeal
1¼ cups (295 ml) whole wheat flour
3 tsp (15 ml) baking powder
½ tsp (3 ml) salt
1 egg, well beaten
½ cup (120 ml) maple syrup
¾ cup (180 ml) skim milk
3 tbsp (45 ml) oil

Mix dry ingredients together. Add remaining ingredients and stir until well blended. Pour into well-greased 9x9-inch pan. Bake at 400°F (205°C) for 20 minutes. Cut into 3-inch squares and serve hot with butter. Yields one loaf.

Approximate nutritional analysis per square:
Calories 216, Protein 5 g, Carbohydrates 37 g, Fat 6 g, Cholesterol 22 mg, Sodium 300 mg

AMARANTH BAKING POWDER BREAD

1 cup (240 ml) amaranth flour
1½ cups (355 ml) brown rice or whole wheat flour
1 tbsp (15 ml) non-alum baking powder
1 tsp (5 ml) sea salt, optional
1 cup (240 ml) milk, soy milk or water
3 tbsp (45 ml) honey
2 tbsp (30 ml) unrefined vegetable oil
2 egg whites

Mix dry and liquid ingredients separately; beat egg whites, then combine all ingredients. Pour batter into well-oiled 8x4-inch pan and bake at 350°F (180°C) about 45 minutes. Cool 10 minutes before removing loaf to rack. Serves 8.

Approximate nutritional analysis per serving:
Calories 268, Protein 8 g, Carbohydrates 47 g, Fat 6 g, Cholesterol 1 mg, Sodium 220 mg

OATMEAL-RAISIN MUFFINS

1 cup (240 ml) buttermilk
1 cup (240 ml) quick oats
1 cup (240 ml) whole wheat flour
1 tsp (5 ml) baking powder
½ tsp (3 ml) baking soda
½ tsp (3 ml) salt
2 tsp (10 ml) cinnamon
⅓ cup (80 ml) softened butter or margarine
¼ cup (60 ml) firmly packed brown sugar
1 tbsp (15 ml) honey
1 egg
½ cup (120 ml) raisins or dried apples, chopped

Boil and stir buttermilk and oats for 2 minutes. Let cool. Preheat oven to 400°F (205°C). Mix flour, baking powder, baking soda, salt and cinnamon in medium bowl. In large bowl cream together butter, brown sugar, honey and egg. Mix in cooled oat mixture. Add raisins. Add dry ingredients and mix with spoon only until dry ingredients are moistened. Fill greased muffin tins ⅔ full. Bake 25-30 minutes. Yields 12 muffins.

Approximate nutritional analysis per muffin:
Calories 157, Protein 4 g, Carbohydrates 23 g, Fat 6 g, Cholesterol 30 mg, Sodium 263 mg

BLUEBERRY-OAT BRAN MUFFINS

1 cup (240 ml) flour
4 tsp (20 ml) non-alum baking powder
½ tsp (3 ml) salt
1 cup (240 ml) oat bran
1 cup (240 ml) blueberries, rinsed
1 cup (240 ml) soy milk
¼ cup (60 ml) unsweetened fruit juice concentrate, any variety
¼ cup (60 ml) melted margarine
2 egg whites, beaten until frothy

Preheat oven to 400°F (205°C). Sift flour, baking powder and salt together into large bowl. Stir in oat bran, then blueberries.

Mix together soy milk, fruit juice concentrate, margarine and egg whites. Combine the two mixtures and stir just enough to moisten ingredients, 12-15 strokes. Grease muffin cups or spray with nonstick cooking spray and fill ⅔ full with batter. Bake 20-25 minutes or until well browned. Yields 12 muffins.

Approximate nutritional analysis per muffin:
Calories 120, Protein 4 g, Carbohydrates 18 g, Fat 5 g, Cholesterol 0 mg, Sodium 300 mg

GLUTEN-FREE ORANGE MUFFINS

1½ cups (355 ml) millet or rice flour
½ cup (120 ml) soy flour
1 tbsp (15 ml) non-alum baking powder
½ tsp (3 ml) sea salt, optional
¼ tsp (1 ml) orange flavoring
1 cup (240 ml) water or orange juice
¼ cup (60 ml) unrefined vegetable oil
¼ cup (60 ml) rice syrup

Combine all dry ingredients. Mix all liquids; add to dry ingredients. Fill muffin cups full and bake at 375°F (190°C) for 15-20 minutes. Yields 12 muffins.

Approximate nutritional analysis per muffin:
Calories 199, Protein 5 g, Carbohydrates 35 g, Fat 6 g, Cholesterol 0 mg, Sodium 123 mg

BANANA MUFFINS

1 cup (240 ml) hazelnut flour
1¼ cups (295 ml) whole wheat flour
2 tsp (10 ml) baking soda
1 tsp (10 ml) cinnamon
½ tsp (3 ml) nutmeg
¼ tsp (1 ml) sea salt
2 free-range eggs
½ cup (120 ml) maple syrup
¼ cup (60 ml) safflower oil
1 tsp (5 ml) vanilla
1⅓ cups (320 ml) mashed banana
¼ cup (60 ml) nonfat yogurt
1 tsp (5 ml) lemon zest

Preheat oven to 375°F (190°C). Combine flours, baking soda, cinnamon, nutmeg and salt. Separately, beat together eggs, maple syrup, oil and vanilla. Stir in banana, yogurt and zest. Add this mixture to dry ingredients and stir until moistened. Fill oiled muffin tins with batter. Bake for 20 minutes. Yields 12 muffins.

Approximate nutritional analysis per muffin:
Calories 196, Protein 8 g, Carbohydrates 28 g, Fat 8 g, Cholesterol 31 mg, Sodium 269 mg

ORANGE-HAZELNUT MUFFINS

1 cup (240 ml) raisins or currants
¾ cup (180 ml) hot water (140°F [60°C])
1 tbsp (15 ml) chopped orange zest
1¾ cups (415 ml) whole wheat flour
1⅓ cups (320 ml) hazelnut flour
1 tbsp (15 ml) baking powder
1 tsp (5 ml) sea salt
½ cup (120 ml) unsalted butter
2 free-range eggs, beaten
1 cup (240 ml) orange juice concentrate
½ cup (120 ml) maple syrup

Soak raisins in hot water and zest overnight; reserve water. Preheat oven to 375°F (188°C). Mix dry ingredients. Cut in butter. Combine eggs, orange juice concentrate and syrup, then add to dry ingredients. Mix in raisins, zest and any remaining soaking water. Do not overmix. Place in oiled muffin tins. Bake at 375°F (190°C) for 20-25 minutes. Yields 12 muffins.

Approximate nutritional analysis per muffin:
Calories 306, Protein 10 g, Carbohydrates 47 g, Fat 11 g, Cholesterol 52 mg, Sodium 314 mg

BLUE CORN-BLUEBERRY MUFFINS

1 cup (240 ml) blue cornmeal
1 cup (240 ml) unbleached white flour
2 tsp (10 ml) non-alum baking powder
½ tsp (3 ml) sea salt, optional
1½ cups (355 ml) water
2-4 tsp (10-20 ml) honey
¼ cup (60 ml) unrefined vegetable oil
1 tsp (5 ml) vanilla
1 cup (240 ml) fresh or frozen blueberries

Stir dry ingredients together. Combine liquid ingredients. Mix liquid and dry ingredients and stir until just mixed. Gently stir in blueberries. Fill oiled muffin tins ⅔ full. Bake in preheated 400°F (205°C) oven for 20 minutes or until done. Yields 12 muffins.

Approximate nutritional analysis per muffin:
Calories 133, Protein 2 g, Carbohydrates 19 g, Fat 5 g, Cholesterol 0 mg, Sodium 82 mg

GRAPE JUICE-SWEETENED CORN MUFFINS

1 cup (240 ml) blue cornmeal
1 cup (240 ml) whole wheat pastry flour
2 tsp (10 ml) non-alum baking powder
¼ tsp (1 ml) sea salt, optional
¼ tsp (1 ml) nutmeg
½ cup (120 ml) chopped nuts
3 tbsp (45 ml) sugar or natural sweetener
1 egg, beaten, or egg replacer
1 tbsp (15 ml) unrefined vegetable oil
¼ cup (60 ml) nonfat plain yogurt
1¼ cups (280 ml) grape juice
1 tsp (5 ml) lemon extract

Combine dry ingredients, and mix in nuts. In separate bowl mix liquids together, then combine with dry ingredients. Batter will seem thin, but it will thicken. Pour batter into oiled muffin tins until ⅔ full. Bake at 425°F (220°C) for 15 minutes. Cool before serving. This recipe can also be used to make pancakes. Yields 12 muffins.

Approximate nutritional analysis per muffin:
Calories 155, Protein 5 g, Carbohydrates 25 g, Fat 5 g, Cholesterol 16 mg, Sodium 92 mg

COLUSA CORN MUFFINS

⅔ cup (160 ml) skim milk
⅓ cup (80 ml) melted butter or margarine
½ cup (120 ml) honey
2 eggs
1½ cups (355 ml) whole wheat flour
⅔ cup (160 ml) cornmeal
2½ tsp (13 ml) baking powder
¼ tsp (1 ml) salt

In small bowl beat together milk, butter, honey and eggs. Set aside. In large bowl stir together dry ingredients. Add honey mixture. Stir just enough to barely moisten flour. Do not overmix. Spoon batter into paper-lined or greased muffin pan cups. Bake at 350°F (180°C) for 20-25 minutes. Serve warm. Yields 18 muffins.

Approximate nutritional analysis per muffin:
Calories 122, Protein 3 g, Carbohydrates 20 g, Fat 4 g, Cholesterol 30 mg, Sodium 144 mg

HONEYED SWEET POTATO BISCUITS

2 cups (480 ml) unbleached flour
1 tbsp (15 ml) baking powder
½ tsp (3 ml) salt
¼ cup (60 ml) shortening
1 tbsp (15 ml) grated orange peel
1 tbsp (15 ml) grated lemon peel
¾ cup (180 ml) baked, peeled and mashed sweet potatoes
⅓ cup (80 ml) honey
½ cup (120 ml) skim milk

In large bowl mix flour, baking powder and salt. Cut in shortening until mixture resembles peas. Add orange and lemon peels, sweet potatoes and honey and mix well. Add enough of the milk to make a soft, but not sticky, dough. Turn out onto floured board and knead three or four times. Pat to 1-inch thickness and cut out 2¼-inch rounds. Place on ungreased cookie sheet and bake at 400°F (205°C) for 15-18 minutes or until lightly browned. Yields 10 biscuits.

Approximate nutritional analysis per biscuit:
Calories 194, Protein 3 g, Carbohydrates 34 g, Fat 5 g, Cholesterol .2 mg, Sodium 270 mg

RAISIN SCONES

2 cups (480 ml) unbleached flour
2 tsp (10 ml) baking powder
2 tbsp (30 ml) granulated raw or turbinado sugar
½ tsp (3 ml) salt
6 tbsp (90 ml) low-fat margarine or butter, cut into small bits
1 cup (240 ml) seedless raisins
½ lemon rind, grated
2 large eggs, well beaten
½ cup (120 ml) plus 1 tbsp (15 ml) skim milk

Preheat oven to 425°F (220°C). Sift flour, baking powder, 1 tbsp sugar and salt into mixing bowl. Add margarine and gently work into flour mixture with hands until coarse crumbs form. Add raisins and lemon rind. Make a well in the dough; add eggs and ½ cup milk. Mix with spoon until dough clumps together. Knead for just 30 seconds then turn onto lightly floured surface. Cut dough in half and form each half into ball. Flatten to form two circles about ¾-inch thick, 5 inches in diameter. Cut each into eight pie-shaped wedges. Place 1 inch apart on lightly greased baking sheet. Brush with 1 tbsp milk and dust with remaining sugar. Bake in center of oven for 12-15 minutes or until lightly browned. Yields 16 scones.

Approximate nutritional analysis per scone:
Calories 116, Protein 2 g, Carbohydrates 22 g, Fat 2 g, Cholesterol .3 mg, Sodium .5 mg

CARROT-BANANA-HONEY WHEAT BREAD

2 pkgs active dry yeast
2¼ cups (540 ml) warm water (105-115°F [41-46°C])
3 cups (720 ml) whole wheat flour
1 cup (240 ml) finely shredded carrots
1 cup (240 ml) mashed ripe bananas
½ cup (120 ml) butter or margarine, softened
⅓ cup (80 ml) honey
1 tbsp (15 ml) salt
½ tsp (3 ml) ground cinnamon
4-6 cups (960-1440 ml) all-purpose flour
2 tbsp (30 ml) butter or margarine, melted

Dissolve yeast in ½ cup warm water in large bowl. Stir in whole wheat flour, remaining 1¾ cups warm water, carrots, bananas, softened butter, honey, salt and cinnamon; beat until smooth using electric mixer. Mix enough all-purpose flour to make soft dough.

Knead dough on lightly floured surface about 10 minutes or until smooth and elastic. Shape dough into ball. Place in greased large bowl; turn to grease all sides. Cover bowl and set in warm place to rise about 1 hour until doubled in bulk.

Punch down dough; divide into two equal pieces. Roll each piece on lightly floured surface into 18x9-inch rectangle. Fold each into thirds to form 6x9-inch rectangle. Roll each piece tightly from 6-inch side, jelly-roll style. Pinch ends and seams to seal; place in greased 9x5x3-inch loaf pan. Brush tops with 2 tbsp melted butter. Cover and set in warm place to rise about 1 hour or until doubled in bulk.

Bake in preheated 375°F (190°C) oven for 40-45 minutes or until loaves sound hollow when tapped and crust is brown. Remove from pans and cool on wire racks. Yields 2 loaves.

Approximate nutritional analysis per slice:
Calories 136, Protein 4 g, Carbohydrates 22 g, Fat 4 g, Cholesterol 10 mg, Sodium 239 mg

MOLASSES-WALNUT WHEAT BREAD

3-3½ cups (720-840 ml) whole wheat flour
1½ tsp (8 ml) salt
1½ tsp (8 ml) cinnamon
1 pkg active dry yeast or quick-rise yeast
¾ cup (180 ml) water
3 tbsp (45 ml) oil
3 tbsp (45 ml) molasses
1½ tsp (8 ml) lemon juice
¼ cup (60 ml) egg whites
½ cup (120 ml) raisins
½ cup (120 ml) chopped walnuts

In large mixing bowl combine 1 cup flour, salt, cinnamon and yeast. Heat water, oil, molasses and lemon juice to 120-130°F (49-54°C). Add to flour mixture; beat with electric mixer 3 minutes on medium speed. Add egg whites, raisins and walnuts; beat 1 minute. By hand, stir in remaining flour to make stiff dough. Turn out onto floured surface, knead until smooth and elastic, about 5-7 minutes. Place in greased bowl, turning to grease top. Cover; let rise in warm place about 1 hour (30 minutes for quick-rise yeast).

Punch down dough. On lightly floured surface, form dough into round loaf. Place on greased cookie sheet. Cover; let rise until doubled, about 1 hour (30 minutes for quick-rise yeast). Bake in preheated 375°F (190°C) oven for 35-40 minutes or until loaf sounds hollow when tapped. Remove from cookie sheet; let cool. Yields 1 loaf.

Approximate nutritional analysis per slice:
Calories 152, Protein 5 g, Carbohydrates 24 g, Fat 5 g, Cholesterol 0 mg, Sodium 210 mg

BEAN & CHILI BREAD

3-3½ cups (720-840 ml) all-purpose flour
½ cup (120 ml) cornmeal
2 tsp (10 ml) chili powder
1 tbsp (15 ml) dried onion flakes
3 tbsp (45 ml) sugar
1 tsp (5 ml) salt
1 pkg active dry yeast or quick-rise yeast
2 tbsp (30 ml) canola oil
1 cup (240 ml) fat-free refried beans
¾ cup (180 ml) plus 1 tbsp (15 ml) water
1 egg white

In large mixing bowl combine 1 cup flour, cornmeal, chili powder, onion flakes, sugar, salt and yeast. Heat oil, refried beans and ¾ cup water to 120-130°F (49-54°C). Add to flour mixture; beat with electric mixer 3 minutes on medium speed. By hand, stir in remaining flour to make firm dough. Turn out onto floured surface; knead until smooth and elastic, about 5-7 minutes. Place in greased bowl, turning to grease top. Cover; let rise in warm place about 1 hour (30 minutes for quick-rise yeast).

Punch down dough. On lightly floured surface, roll dough into 7x15-inch rectangle. Starting with shorter side, roll up tightly, pressing dough into roll with each turn. Pinch edges and ends to seal. Place in greased 9x5-inch loaf pan. Cover; let rise until double, about 45 minutes (30 minutes for quick-rise yeast). Brush top of loaf with mixture of egg white and 1 tbsp water. Sprinkle generously with dried onion flakes. Bake in preheated 375°F (190°C) oven for 20-25 minutes or until loaf sounds hollow when tapped. Remove from pan and cool. Yields 1 loaf.

Approximate nutritional analysis per slice:
Calories 162, Protein 5 g, Carbohydrates 30 g, Fat 2 g, Cholesterol 0 mg, Sodium 271 mg

DUTCH DOUBLE DILL BREAD

1 pkg active dry yeast
2 cups (480 ml) warm water (105-115°F [41-46°C])
2 tbsp (30 ml) salad oil
3 tbsp (45 ml) honey
1 cup (240 ml) plain yogurt or dairy sour cream
2 tsp (10 ml) salt
1 tbsp (15 ml) dill weed
1 tbsp (15 ml) dill seeds
5 cups (1.2 l) whole wheat flour
3 cups (720 ml) rye flour

In small bowl combine yeast and ½ cup warm water. Set aside for 5-10 minutes. Combine remaining water, salad oil, honey, yogurt, salt, dill weed and dill seeds in large bowl. Add yeast mixture, then whole wheat flour, 1 cup at a time, stirring well after each addition. Add rye flour until mixture becomes too difficult to stir. Begin kneading, adding additional flour to keep the dough from becoming too sticky. Knead for at least 10 minutes. Shape into ball. Lightly grease clean mixing bowl. Place dough in bowl, turning to grease the top. Cover. Let rise in warm, draft-free place until doubled in size.

    Punch down. Turn dough out onto lightly floured board. Knead 1 minute. Shape into round loaves or place in greased 9x5x3-inch loaf pans. Cover. Let rise in warm, draft-free place until loaves are doubled in size, about 30 minutes. Bake at 425°F (220°C) for 15 minutes. Reduce heat to 350°F (180°C). Bake another 25-30 minutes or until bread sounds hollow when tapped. Yields 2 large loaves.

Approximate nutritional analysis per slice:
Calories 117, Protein 4 g, Carbohydrates 23 g, Fat 2 g, Cholesterol 1 mg, Sodium 138 mg

RAISED MULTIGRAIN CORN BREAD

½ cup (120 ml) yellow cornmeal
½ cup (120 ml) rolled oats
½ cup (120 ml) 100% bran cereal
¼ cup (60 ml) wheat germ
2 cups (480 ml) boiling water
2 pkgs active dry yeast
½ cup (120 ml) warm water (115-120°F [46-49°C])
⅓ cup (80 ml) honey
2 tbsp (30 ml) butter or margarine, melted
1 tsp (5 ml) salt
2 cups (480 ml) whole wheat flour
3 cups (720 ml) unbleached flour

In 1-quart glass measuring cup or bowl, combine cornmeal, oats, bran and wheat germ. Pour in boiling water. Stir thoroughly. Set aside to cool. Place yeast in large mixing bowl. Add warm water. Stir to dissolve yeast. Add honey, butter and salt. Mix thoroughly. Add cooled cornmeal mixture. Stir until smooth. Stir in whole wheat flour. Gradually add unbleached flour, 1 cup at a time, until mixture is stiff enough to knead, about 2½ cups. Sprinkle remaining flour on board. Knead dough for 10-12 minutes until smooth. Add additional flour as necessary. Shape dough into ball. Lightly grease clean mixing bowl. Place dough in warm, draft-free place until doubled in size, about 1½ hours.

Punch dough down to remove air bubbles. Turn out onto lightly floured board. Divide dough in half. Shape each half into round loaf. Place loaves on large, lightly greased cookie sheet or two pie plates. Cover. Place in warm, draft-free place until doubled in size, about 1 hour. Bake in preheated 350°F (180°C) oven for 40-50 minutes or until bread sounds hollow when tapped. Remove loaves from cookie sheet. Cool on wire racks. Yields 2 loaves.

Approximate nutritional analysis per slice:
Calories 105, Protein 3 g, Carbohydrates 21 g, Fat 1 g, Cholesterol 2 mg, Sodium 82 mg

SWEDISH RYE BREAD

2 cups (480 ml) milk, scalded and cooled
2 tsp (10 ml) salt
1-2 tbsp (15-30 ml) caraway seeds
¼ cup (60 ml) maple syrup
2 tbsp (30 ml) mild molasses
1 pkg active dry yeast dissolved in ¼ cup (60 ml)
    warm water (115-120°F [46-49°C])
2 cups (480 ml) rye flour
3 tbs (45 ml) oil or melted shortening
3-4 cups (720-960 ml) white flour

Combine milk, salt, caraway seeds, maple syrup and molasses in mixing bowl. Add yeast (dissolved in water) and rye flour. Beat until smooth, about 75 strokes. Cover, let stand until bubbly and foamy, 1-2 hours or overnight. Stir down; add oil. Gradually work in white flour until stiff dough is formed. Knead thoroughly until smooth. Let rise until doubled in bulk. Punch down, let rise again until doubled. Divide dough and place in two greased 9x5x3-inch loaf pans. Bake at 375°F (190°C) about 35-40 minutes, until loaf sounds hollow when tapped. Remove from pans and cool on rack. Yields 2 medium loaves, 16 slices per loaf.

Approximate nutritional analysis per slice:
Calories 94, Protein 2 g, Carbohydrates 17 g, Fat 2 g, Cholesterol 1 mg, Sodium 142 mg

QUICK BUNS

1¾ cups (415 ml) warm water (115-120°F [46-49°C])
½ cup (120 ml) oil
¼ cup (60 ml), heaping, sugar
3 tbsp (45 ml) yeast
1½ tsp (8 ml) salt
2 eggs
5¼ cups (1.3 l) whole wheat flour

Mix together water, oil, sugar and yeast and let stand 15 minutes. Add salt, eggs and flour. Mix well and shape into buns. Let stand 15 minutes. Bake at 425°F (220°C) for 10 minutes. Yields 24 buns.

Approximate nutritional analysis per bun:
Calories 145, Protein 4 g, Carbohydrates 22 g, Fat 5 g, Cholesterol 16 mg, Sodium 140 mg

WHOLE WHEAT CRESCENT ROLLS

½ cup (120 ml) honey
½ cup (120 ml) hot water (140°F [60°C])
2 tbsp (30 ml) yeast
½ cup (120 ml) dry potato flakes
1½ cups (355 ml) warm water (115-120°F [46-49°C])
1 tsp (5 ml) salt
3 tbsp (45 ml) shortening
⅔ cup (160 ml) dry instant milk
5-5½ cups (1.2-1.3 l) whole wheat flour
½ cup (120 ml) softened butter or margarine

In small bowl dissolve honey in hot water. Stir in yeast. Let stand 15 minutes. Mix together potato flakes, warm water, salt, shortening and dry milk. Mix in 2 cups of the flour. Beat 5 minutes. Add yeast mixture and beat 1 minute longer. Add remaining flour. Knead until smooth and elastic.

Divide dough in half. On lightly floured surface roll each half into a 12-inch circle. Spread ¼ cup margarine on each circle. Cut each circle into 12 wedges. Roll each wedge, starting with wide edge and rolling toward point. Place point down on greased baking sheet about 2 inches apart. Let sit for 20 minutes. Bake at 350°F (180°C) for 12-15 minutes. Yields 24 rolls.

Approximate nutritional analysis per roll:
Calories 166, Protein 4 g, Carbohydrates 26 g, Fat 6 g, Cholesterol 11 mg, Sodium 141 mg

HOLIDAY DINNER ROLLS

2 tbsp (30 ml) dry yeast
¾ cup (180 ml) warm water (115-120°F [46-49°C])
¼ cup (60 ml) honey
¼ tsp (1 ml) sea salt, optional
¼ cup (60 ml) vegetable oil plus enough water to make
   ⅓ cup (80 ml) liquid
1 egg or ¼ cup (60 ml) egg replacer
½ cup (120 ml) prepared potato flakes
1½ cups (355 ml) whole wheat flour
2 cups (480 ml) unbleached white flour

Dissolve yeast in warm water in large bowl. Leave until bubbly, about 10 minutes. Add honey, salt, oil, egg, potato flakes and half of flours. Beat thoroughly. Add enough flour to make manageable dough. Turn out onto lightly floured board and knead for 10 minutes until dough is smooth and elastic. Place in lightly oiled bowl, turning once to coat. Set in warm place and let rise for 1 hour.

   Punch down, turn onto floured board and shape into desired shape of roll. Place rolls on greased cookie sheet. Cover lightly with plastic or cotton towel and place in warm place to rise until light, about 20-30 minutes. Bake at 375°F (190°C) for 15-20 minutes. Yields 24 rolls.

Approximate nutritional analysis per roll:
Calories 101, Protein 3 g, Carbohydrates 17 g, Fat 3 g, Cholesterol 8 mg, Sodium 4 mg

TOASTED AMARANTH ROLLS

1½ cups (355 ml) warm water (105-115°F [41-46°C])
1½ tbsp (25 ml) unrefined vegetable oil
3 tbs (45 ml) honey or maple syrup
1½ tsp (8 ml) sea salt, optional
1½ tsp (8 ml) active dry yeast
1 cup (240 ml) amaranth flour
2¼ cups (540 ml) whole wheat flour
soft butter, optional
honey, optional
cinnamon, optional
chopped nuts, raisins, dried lemon peel, optional
toasted amaranth seeds, optional

Mix first five ingredients together, then stir in flours. Roll dough onto lightly floured surface, about ¼ inch thick. Brush with butter and sprinkle with remaining ingredients, except amaranth seeds. Toast seeds in dry skillet until lightly browned. Roll up dough and slice 2 inches thick. Place on sides, close together in oiled pan. Sprinkle with amaranth seeds and bake at 350°F (180°C) for 30-40 minutes. Yields 24 rolls.

Approximate nutritional analysis per roll:
Calories 85, Protein 3 g, Carbohydrates 16 g, Fat 2 g, Cholesterol 0 mg, Sodium 3 mg

AMARANTH RYE STICKS

1 pkg active dry yeast
1½ cups (355 ml) warm water(105-115°F [41-46°C])
1 tbsp (15 ml) nonfat dry milk
1 tbsp (15 ml) molasses
½ tsp (3 ml) sea salt, optional
3¼ cups (780 ml) rye flour
½ cup (120 ml) amaranth flour
1 tsp (5 ml) caraway seeds
sesame seeds, optional

Dissolve yeast in warm water; stir in milk, molasses and salt. Add flours. Stir in caraway seeds. Knead dough about 5 minutes. Cut into 36 pieces and roll into sticks approximately 5 inches long. Roll in sesame seeds. Place on an oiled baking sheet, spray with water, then bake at 425°F (220°C) for 18-20 minutes or until lightly browned. Yields 36 sticks.

Approximate nutritional analysis per stick:
Calories 45, Protein 1 g, Carbohydrates 9 g, Fat .4 g, Cholesterol 0 mg, Sodium 2 mg

WHOLE WHEAT PIZZA CRUST

1 tbsp (15 ml) active dry yeast
1½ cups (355 ml) warm water (105-115°F [41-46°C])
3 cups (720 ml) whole wheat flour
1½ tsp (8 ml) salt
1 tsp (5 ml) honey
cornmeal, optional

Dissolve yeast in water. Mix together all ingredients, except cornmeal. Beat vigorously with fork until smooth. Let rise until double. Shape into two greased pizza, or 11x14½-inch, pans. Lightly oil dough before putting on sauce to prevent dough from becoming soggy. Bake topped pizza at 425°F (220°C) for 20 minutes. Yields 2 crusts.

For crispier crust sprinkle cornmeal on greased pan before laying down dough.

Approximate nutritional analysis per slice w/o topping:
Calories 79, Protein 3 g, Carbohydrates 17 g, Fat .4 g, Cholesterol 0 mg, Sodium 201 mg

Starters & Snacks

ROSEMARY-VEGETABLE FOCACCIA BREAD

1 lb (455 g) frozen bread dough, thawed
olive oil spray
1 tbsp (15 ml) finely chopped fresh rosemary
½ onion, minced
½ cup (120 ml) prepared pasta sauce
2 zucchini, thinly sliced
½ lb (230 g) mushrooms, sliced
½ cup (120 ml) chopped red bell pepper
½ cup (120 ml) chopped green pepper
3 tomatoes, thinly sliced
¼ cup (60 ml) grated Parmesan cheese

Place bread dough on lightly floured surface. Flatten slightly and spray with olive oil spray. Sprinkle with fresh rosemary and onion and knead well to mix thoroughly. Roll out dough to 9x6-inch rectangle. Spray 12x9-inch baking pan with olive oil spray. Press dough out until it fills pan. Bake at 400°F (205°C) for 10 minutes. Remove bread from oven. Top with sauce, then layer zucchini, mushrooms and peppers. Top with tomatoes and cheese. Return to oven and bake 10-15 minutes. Serves 12.

Approximate nutritional analysis per serving:
Calories 136, Protein 5 g, Carbohydrates 24 g, Fat 2 g, Cholesterol 3 mg, Sodium 295 mg

SHRIMP WONTONS

3 tbsp (45 ml) oil
1 medium onion, minced
1 clove garlic, minced
½ lb (230 g) tofu, diced
½ lb (230 g) shrimp or chicken, diced
¼ cup (60 ml) bread crumbs
3 tbsp (45 ml) soy sauce
1 egg, beaten
12-oz pkg (360 g) wonton wrappers (40 wrappers)

Heat oil in skillet to medium heat. Sauté onion and garlic until transparent. Add tofu and shrimp or chicken. Sauté for 3 minutes. Take mixture out of skillet. Place in bowl with bread crumbs; add soy sauce and beaten egg and mix together. Place 1 teaspoon of mixture into each wonton wrapper and deep fry until golden brown; or drop into soup and simmer for 5 minutes. Yields 40 wontons.

Approximate nutritional analysis per wonton:
Calories 50, Protein 3 g, Carbohydrates 6 g, Fat 2 g, Cholesterol 17 mg, Sodium 146 mg

STUFFED SHIITAKE MUSHROOMS

2 cups (480 ml) brown jasmine rice
4 cups (960 ml) water
2 lbs (910 g) fresh shiitake or regular mushrooms
2 tsp (10 ml) olive oil
1 tbsp (15 ml) butter
¾ cup (180 ml) finely chopped red onion
1 cup (240 ml) finely chopped green pepper
2 tsp (10 ml) dried basil
5 tbsp (75 ml) nonfat cream cheese
fresh parsley, optional

Cook rice in water as directed. Set aside. Clean mushrooms; discard stems if using shiitake mushrooms. In large skillet sauté mushrooms in olive oil and butter until golden brown on both sides; set aside. Sauté onion, green pepper and basil until onion is golden. Stir in rice, cream cheese and salt and pepper to taste. Preheat oven to 350°F (180°C). Arrange mushrooms, rib side up, on rimmed cookie sheet. Divide rice mixture among mushrooms. Bake just until mushrooms are reheated, about 10 minutes. Top each with parsley sprig. Serves 10.

Approximate nutritional analysis per serving:
Calories 205, Protein 6 g, Carbohydrates 40 g, Fat 3 g, Cholesterol 5 mg, Sodium 94 mg

BLINI

Russian Appetizer Pancakes

2 cups (480 ml) milk
1 tbsp (15 ml) sugar
1 pkg active dry yeast
2 cups (480 ml) all-purpose flour
2 tbsp (30 ml) melted butter or margarine
3 eggs, separated
¾ tsp (4 ml) salt
½ cup (120 ml) buckwheat flour

Scald milk and pour into large bowl. When lukewarm, add sugar and yeast, mixing well to dissolve yeast. Stir in 1 cup of all-purpose flour; cover bowl and set in warm place until "sponge" doubles in volume, about 1½ hours. Combine butter, egg yolks and salt. Stir down sponge and add butter-egg mixture, along with buckwheat flour and remaining 1 cup of all-purpose flour. Beat egg whites until stiff but not dry, then gently fold into batter. Cook batter, 1 tablespoon per blini, on hot, buttered griddle or skillet. Flip blini to brown second side after batter appears set on top. Cover blini with towel and hold in 200°F (93°C) oven until serving. Accompany blini with caviar, smoked salmon, minced onion, sour cream or yogurt cheese. Yields 40 blini.

Approximate nutritional analysis per blini w/o accompaniments:
Calories 44, Protein 2 g, Carbohydrates 7 g, Fat 1 g, Cholesterol 16 mg, Sodium 57 mg

GARBANZO-POTATO PANCAKES

1 cup (240 ml) garbanzo flour
1 cup (240 ml) potato flakes
½ tsp (3 ml) sea salt, optional
2 tsp (10 ml) non-alum baking powder
½ cup (120 ml) finely chopped onion
1 medium zucchini squash or cucumber, grated
2 cups (480 ml) water

VARIATION:
½ cup (120 ml) whole wheat flour
1 tbsp (15 ml) oil
2 tsp (10 ml) tamari sauce
garlic

Mix the dry ingredients and the vegetables together. Add the water and stir well. Cook like pancakes on an oiled skillet or griddle. Yields 12 pancakes.

Variation: For lighter, extra-tasty pancakes, substitute the whole wheat flour for ½ cup of the potato flakes. Add oil, tamari sauce and a little garlic to the water and stir into the dry mixture. Cook as directed.

Approximate nutritional analysis per pancake:
Calories 60, Protein 3 g, Carbohydrates 11 g, Fat .9 g, Cholesterol 0 mg, Sodium 90 mg

Approximate nutritional analysis per pancake variation:
Calories 81, Protein 3 g, Carbohydrates 14 g, Fat 2 g, Cholesterol 0 mg, Sodium 146 mg

WHITE BEAN PURÉE

14-oz can (420 g) great northern beans, rinsed and drained
2 tbsp (30 ml) chopped onion
1 tsp (5 ml) finely chopped garlic
¼ tsp (1 ml) sea salt
1 tbsp (15 ml) lemon juice
2 tsp (10 ml) olive oil
hot pepper sauce, optional

In food processor or blender combine first six ingredients and blend until smooth, 60-90 seconds. Add hot pepper sauce to taste. Transfer to serving bowl, cover and refrigerate 2 hours. Serve with toasted pita bread or other crispy bread. Yields 1 cup.

Approximate nutritional analysis per 2-tbsp serving:
Calories 70, Protein 4 g, Carbohydrates 11 g, Fat 1 g, Cholesterol 0 mg, Sodium 68 mg

ANASAZI BEAN SPREAD

1 cup (240 ml) anasazi beans, cooked
½ medium onion
1 stalk celery
¼ cup (60 ml) tofu, drained
1 tbsp (15 ml) unrefined olive oil
½ tsp (3 ml) vegetable salt substitute
½ tsp (3 ml) chili powder
½ tsp (3 ml) oregano
½ tsp (3 ml) basil
¼ tsp (1 ml) garlic powder

Blend all ingredients together in blender or food processor until smooth. Great for dips or sandwich spread. Serves 8.

Approximate nutritional analysis per serving:
Calories 50, Protein 2 g, Carbohydrates 6 g, Fat 2 g, Cholesterol 0 mg, Sodium 132 mg

BLACK BEAN DIP WITH MARJORAM

2 15-oz cans (900 g) low-sodium black beans, drained
1 cup (240 ml) diced white onion
1 tbsp (15 ml) chopped garlic
1 tbsp (15 ml) chili powder
¼ tsp (1 ml) white pepper
1 tbsp (15 ml) cumin
water
2 cups (480 ml) nonfat plain yogurt
4 tbsp (60 ml) chopped fresh marjoram
3 cups (720 ml) jicama sticks
2½ cups (590 ml) celery sticks
2½ cups (590 ml) carrot sticks

In food processor blend beans, onion, garlic, chili powder, white pepper and cumin until smooth, adding water until desired consistency is reached. Remove to bowl and fold in yogurt and marjoram. Serve with jicama, celery and carrot sticks. Serves 8.

Approximate nutritional analysis per serving:
Calories 236, Protein 13 g, Carbohydrates 41 g, Fat 3 g, Cholesterol 1 mg, Sodium 109 mg

BLACK-EYED PEA HABAÑERO DIP

11-oz pkg (330 g) black-eyed peas, cooked and drained
⅓ cup (80 ml) chopped rehydrated dried tomatoes
⅓ cup (80 ml) chopped red or green bell pepper
¼ cup (60 ml) minced red onion
1 clove elephant garlic, peeled and chopped
2 tbsp (30 ml) minced fresh cilantro leaves
1 dried habañero chile, reconstituted, seeded and finely chopped
fresh cilantro, chopped tomato or red onion, for garnish

In blender or food processor blend all ingredients until smooth. Garnish as desired. Serve with tortilla chips, jicama sticks or other fresh vegetables. Yields 2½ cups.

Approximate nutritional analysis per ½-cup serving:
Calories 232, Protein 16 g, Carbohydrates 42 g, Fat .9 g, Cholesterol 0 mg, Sodium 86 mg

MINTED VEGETABLE DIP

1¼ cups (295 ml) nonfat plain yogurt
¾ cup (180 ml) light sour cream
3 cloves garlic, minced
1 cucumber, peeled, seeded and chopped
1 tbsp (15 ml) chopped fresh mint
8 cups (1.9 l) assorted raw vegetable sticks or florets

Put first five ingredients into food processor or blender and process until very well combined. Salt and pepper to taste. Chill. Serve with raw vegetables. Serves 8.

Approximate nutritional analysis per 1 cup vegetables and ¼ cup dip:
Calories 93, Protein 6 g, Carbohydrates 15 g, Fat 2 g, Cholesterol 8 mg, Sodium 155 mg

MINTED TOFU DIP

2 tbsp (30 ml) minced fresh mint
10-oz pkg (300 g) silken tofu, firm, drained
1 tbsp (15 ml) lemon juice
2½ tsp (13 ml) minced garlic
¼ tsp (1 ml) pepper
¼ cup (60 ml) chopped green onion
½ cup (120 ml) chopped water chestnuts, optional
salt to taste, optional

In food processor or blender combine first six ingredients until smooth. Whirl 30 seconds on high. Stir in water chestnuts and salt to taste. Refrigerate 1 hour. Serve as dip with raw vegetables or mound on your favorite greens. Top with diced tomatoes or pimiento. Yields 2½ cups.

Approximate nutritional analysis per ¼-cup serving:
Calories 42, Protein 3 g, Carbohydrates 6 g, Fat 1 g, Cholesterol 0 mg, Sodium 36 mg

DOLMAS
Stuffed Grape Leaves

¼ lb (115 g) lean ground lamb
1 cup (240 ml) chopped onion
2 cloves garlic, minced
2 tbsp (30 ml) olive oil
1 cup (240 ml) kasha, medium granulation
1 egg, slightly beaten
¼ cup (60 ml) minced fresh parsley
1 tsp (5 ml) dried dill weed
1 tsp (5 ml) crushed dried mint leaves
½ tsp (3 ml) ground coriander
¼ tsp (1 ml) cinnamon
2½ cups (590 ml) hot, seasoned chicken broth
½ cup (120 ml) fresh lemon juice
1-lb jar (455 g) grape leaves in brine

In large skillet sauté lamb, onion and garlic in oil just until meat loses its pinkness. Combine kasha with egg, then add to skillet along with herbs and spices, 1 cup of broth and ¼ cup of lemon juice. Simmer, covered, 5 minutes; remove from heat and cool. Plunge grape leaves briefly into hot water to separate them, then drain. On clean, flat surface, place leaf shiny side down, trim and discard stem. Spoon 2-4 tbsp filling at stem end, fold sides of leaves over filling and roll up. Arrange dolmas, touching each other, in oiled 7x11-inch baking dish, forming two layers. Pour remaining broth and lemon juice over dolmas, cover dish with foil and weight top with heat-proof pan or dish to keep dolmas from unwinding.

Bake at 325°F (165°C) for 60 minutes. Turn heat off but leave dolmas in oven 30 minutes more. Remove from cooking liquid before serving warm or chilled. Yields 50 dolmas.

Note: Stuffed unbaked dolmas can be frozen up to 3 months.

Approximate nutritional analysis per stuffed grape leaf:
Calories 22, Protein 1 g, Carbohydrates 2 g, Fat 1 g, Cholesterol 6 mg, Sodium 44 mg

Soups

ROASTED PEPPER & YOGURT SOUP

1¾ lbs (795 g) red bell peppers
1¼ lbs (570 g) yellow bell peppers
2 cups (480 ml) nonfat plain yogurt
1 cup (240 ml) chicken stock
1 tbsp (15 ml) chopped fresh chervil
1 tbsp (15 ml) chopped fresh tarragon
1 tbsp (15 ml) chopped fresh basil
½ tsp (3 ml) salt
white pepper
1 tbsp (15 ml) balsamic vinegar
1 lb (455 g) tiny salad shrimp, peeled, deveined and poached,
*   or small scallops, poached*
nonfat plain yogurt mixed with more chervil,
*   tarragon and basil, for garnish*

Preheat the broiler and place the broiler rack as close to the heat as possible. Use aluminum foil to line a cookie sheet with sides. Place washed and dried bell peppers on the foil and broil them, turning them with tongs every few minutes until they are charred all over. Be careful not to break the skins. Remove the charred peppers to a large bowl or bowls and let them cool.

When the peppers are cool, place a colander over a large bowl. Peel the peppers, catching the peeled peppers in the colander and the juices in the bowl. Discard the seeds and blackened skins.

Transfer the peppers and their juices to the bowl of a food processor fitted with a steel blade. Purée until smooth, then strain the purée through a sieve. Return the strained mixture to the food processor with the steel blade in place. Add the yogurt, chicken stock, chopped herbs, salt, pepper to taste and vinegar. Process until blended. Chill.

Serve very cold, poured over the poached shrimp or scallops in individual soup bowls. Garnish with yogurt-mixed chervil, tarragon and basil. Serves 6.

Approximate nutritional analysis per serving:
Calories 231, Protein 26 g, Carbohydrates 22 g, Fat 4 g, Cholesterol 140 mg, Sodium 750 mg

CREAMY BLUEBERRY BISQUE

2 cups (480 ml) fresh blueberries
2 cups (480 ml) water
⅓ cup (80 ml) granulated sugar
1 tbsp (15 ml) brown sugar
1 cinnamon stick
1 lemon, thinly sliced
2 cups (480 ml) nonfat plain yogurt
1 cup (240 ml) apple juice
nonfat plain yogurt, for garnish

Reserve a few blueberries for garnish. Place the remaining blueberries, water, sugars, cinnamon and lemon in a saucepan. Simmer, uncovered, for 15 minutes, then drain through a sieve into a bowl underneath. Chill the sieved liquid. Just before serving, whisk together the liquid, yogurt and apple juice. Garnish each serving with a spoonful of yogurt and a few berries. Serves 6.

Approximate nutritional analysis per serving:
Calories 141, Protein 5 g, Carbohydrates 31 g, Fat .4 g, Cholesterol 1 mg, Sodium 67 mg

STRAWBERRY SOUP

10-oz pkg (300 g) frozen unsweetened strawberries, thawed
2 tsp (10 ml) sugar
juice of ½ lemon
½ tsp (3 ml) almond extract
1 cup (240 ml) low-fat strawberry yogurt
8 oz (240 ml) champagne

Purée the strawberries in a blender or food processor. Add the sugar, lemon juice and almond extract, then the yogurt and champagne. Blend until very smooth. Chill for at least 3 hours. Serve cold in small dessert dishes or cups with saucers. Serves 6.

Note: For a thicker soup, use 2 cups of yogurt.

Approximate nutritional analysis per serving:
Calories 93, Protein 2 g, Carbohydrates 14 g, Fat .5 g, Cholesterol 2 mg, Sodium 27 mg

COLD TOMATO-DILL SOUP

2 tbsp (30 ml) olive oil
2-3 medium onions, chopped
2-4 cloves garlic, crushed
6-8 tomatoes, peeled and chopped
2 cups (480 ml) chicken stock
½ tsp (3 ml) white pepper
3 tbsp (45 ml) finely chopped fresh dill, or 1½ tsp (8 ml) dried dill
1 tsp (5 ml) sugar
2 cups (480 ml) nonfat plain yogurt
1 cup (240 ml) buttermilk or skim milk
nonfat plain yogurt, for garnish
dill or chives, chopped, for garnish

Heat the olive oil in a skillet over medium heat. Add the onions and garlic and sauté until soft but not brown. Add the tomatoes, chicken stock, pepper and dill. Cover and simmer for 15 minutes.

Cool the cooked mixture slightly, then process in a blender or food processor in batches. Add the sugar, yogurt and milk to the tomato mixture. Blend well. Chill. Adjust the seasonings, pour into individual bowls and garnish each with a dollop of yogurt sprinkled with chopped dill or chives. Serve very cold. Serves 8.

Note: Can be frozen before adding the sugar, yogurt and milk. After thawing, proceed with the recipe.

Approximate nutritional analysis per serving:
Calories 119, Protein 7 g, Carbohydrates 14 g, Fat 4 g, Cholesterol 2 mg, Sodium 282 mg

CUCUMBER-YOGURT SOUP

4 medium to large cucumbers, peeled
fresh mint sprigs
2 cups (480 ml) skim milk
2 cups (480 ml) nonfat plain yogurt
1-2 tbsp (15-30 ml) honey
1 tsp (5 ml) chopped fresh dill
2-3 scallions, chopped

Reserve a few cucumber slices and whole mint leaves for garnish. Chop the remaining cucumbers into large pieces, then purée them with the remaining mint and all other ingredients in a blender or food processor, adding salt and pepper to taste. Chill for several hours. Serve cold, garnished with the reserved cucumber slices and mint leaves.. Serves 6.

Approximate nutritional analysis per serving:
Calories 112, Protein 9 g, Carbohydrates 19 g, Fat .6 g, Cholesterol 3 mg, Sodium 109 mg

GARNET YAM SOUP

3 medium carrots, sliced into uniform pieces
½ medium yellow onion, sliced into uniform pieces
1-2 tbsp (15-30 ml) olive oil
3 medium garnet yams, cut into large pieces
1 small potato, sliced into uniform pieces
2 tbsp (30 ml) soy sauce
1 tsp (5 ml) basil
cayenne

Sauté carrots and onion for 2-3 minutes in olive oil. Add yams and potato and cover with water. Simmer for 15-20 minutes until yams are soft. Add soy sauce, basil and cayenne and salt to taste. Blend or food process until creamy. Add more water to adjust thickness. Serves 6.

Approximate nutritional analysis per serving:
Calories 260, Protein 5 g, Carbohydrates 55 g, Fat 3 g, Cholesterol 0 mg, Sodium 377 mg

YELLOW POTATO-LEEK SOUP

3 stalks celery, sliced
1 medium white onion, thinly sliced
2 medium leeks, sliced then rinsed
3 garlic cloves, sliced
2 tbsp (30 ml) olive oil
3 medium yellow finn potatoes, unpeeled,
   cut into uniform chunks
3 large red potatoes, cut into uniform chunks
pinch chopped fresh parsley
2 tsp (10 ml) basil
2 bay leaves
2 tsp (10 ml) cumin
3 tbsp (45 ml) shoyu sauce
½ tsp (3 ml) black pepper
pinch chopped fresh dill

Sauté celery, onion, leeks and garlic in oil for 2-3 minutes. Combine all ingredients, except fresh dill, in stockpot and cover with water. Simmer for 30-45 minutes or until potatoes are soft. Reserving ½-1 cup vegetables, blend soup into purée using blender, food processor or potato ricer (for more texture). Combine fresh dill and reserved vegetables with purée. Reheat and serve. Serves 6.

Approximate nutritional analysis per serving:
Calories 280, Protein 6 g, Carbohydrates 55 g, Fat 5 g, Cholesterol 0 mg, Sodium 551 mg

CURRY MUSHROOM SOUP

light vegetable oil spray
2 leeks, sliced and diced
pinch curry powder
2 twists fresh pepper from pepper mill
2 tbsp (30 ml) flour
1 cup (240 ml) beef stock
1 cup (240 ml) skim milk
6 mushrooms (2 shiitake, 2 portobello, 2 regular), sliced
½ cup (120 ml) chopped parsley

Lightly spray bottom of soup pot with vegetable oil. Sauté leeks until tender. Add curry powder and pepper. Add flour and stir until blended. Add beef stock. Stir well. Add milk. Stir well. Simmer until reduced by half. Add sliced mushrooms. Simmer very gently for 5 minutes. Pour into bowls and top with chopped parsley. Serves 2.

Approximate nutritional analysis per ¾-cup serving:
Calories 186, Protein 10 g, Carbohydrates 34 g, Fat 2 g, Cholesterol 2 mg, Sodium 134 mg

CREAMY TOMATO-ONION SOUP

¾ cup (180 ml) chopped onions
3 tbsp (45 ml) defatted chicken stock
2 cups (480 ml) puréed fresh or canned unsalted tomatoes
1 tsp (5 ml) sweet basil
2 medium garlic cloves, pressed, or 1 tbsp (15 ml) garlic powder
¼ tsp (1 ml) coarsely ground pepper
10½-oz pkg (315 g) light tofu, drained
pinch salt, optional

In medium saucepan sauté onions in chicken stock until transparent. Add puréed tomatoes along with next three ingredients. Simmer 10-15 minutes. In blender or food processor process tofu until smooth and stir into tomato mixture. Add salt. Simmer and serve hot. Serves 3.

Approximate nutritional analysis per 8-oz serving:
Calories 101, Protein 7 g, Carbohydrates 13 g, Fat 3 g, Cholesterol 0 mg, Sodium 14 mg

CREAM OF SQUASH-CILANTRO SOUP

SAFETY TIP: Be careful when blending hot ingredients in a closed blender because they will explode with the pressure from the heat. Start the blender on low with the lid slightly open, then turn to high speed and seal the lid, or use a hand blender and blend the soup in the cooking pot.

> **2 tbsp (30 ml) extra-virgin olive oil**
> **4 cups (960 ml) peeled and cubed buttercup or other winter squash**
>   **or carrots**
> **2 cups (480 ml) chopped onion**
> **1 cup (240 ml) thinly sliced celery**
> **¼ cup (60 ml) chopped fresh cilantro**
> **2 tbsp (30 ml) minced fresh garlic**
> **4 cups (960 ml) water**
> **1 tsp (5 ml) sea salt**
> **¼ tsp (1 ml) coriander powder**
> **½ cup (120 ml) soy milk powder**

Warm a large skillet on medium heat for 30 seconds, then add the oil, squash, onion, celery, cilantro and garlic. Sauté for about 10 minutes, then add the water, sea salt and coriander. Cook, covered, until the squash is done, then transfer to a blender. Add the soy milk powder, then blend for about 30 seconds or until the soup is mostly smooth with some small chunks. Serve hot. Serves 4.

Approximate nutritional analysis per serving:
Calories 249, Protein 6 g, Carbohydrates 37 g, Fat 10 g, Cholesterol 0 mg, Sodium 629 mg

SWEET CORN SOUP

2 qts (1.9 l) spring water
¼ cup (60 ml) wakame
4 ears fresh sweet corn, kernels removed and reserved
2 onions, diced
1 tsp (5 ml) safflower or light sesame oil
½ tsp (3 ml) sea salt
½ cup (120 ml) cooked brown rice
¼ cup (60 ml) light miso
parsley or cilantro, for garnish

In large pot add water, wakame and bare corn cobs. Bring to boil, simmer 20 minutes and remove cobs. Meanwhile, sauté onions in oil and sea salt. Next, add sautéed onions, corn kernels and rice to stock and simmer for 30 minutes. Dissolve miso in ½ cup of soup stock and add to soup. Simmer on low for 2 minutes and stir. Place in bowls and garnish with parsley or cilantro. Serves 8.

Approximate nutritional analysis per serving:
Calories 94, Protein 3 g, Carbohydrates 19 g, Fat 2 g, Cholesterol 0 mg, Sodium 442 mg

CREAM OF ASPARAGUS SOUP

1 lb (455 g) fresh asparagus, cut into 1-inch pieces
1 cup (240 ml) water
½ cup (120 ml) chopped onion
2 tbsp (30 ml) butter
4 cups (960 ml) chicken stock
1 tbsp (15 ml) unbleached all-purpose flour
2 cups (480 ml) nonfat plain yogurt
cayenne pepper

Separate the asparagus tips from the stalks. Simmer the tips in water 5 minutes, then drain and reserve. Sauté the onion in 1 tbsp butter. Add the asparagus stalks and sauté briefly. Add 3½ cups chicken stock, bring to a boil and simmer for 5-8 minutes, or until the asparagus is tender. Purée the vegetable-stock mixture in a blender, then return it to the pan.

In a separate pan melt the remaining 1 tbsp butter and blend in the flour; gradually blend in ½ cup of the stock. Add this mixture to the vegetable-stock mixture and mix thoroughly. Simmer for 1 minute. Add more stock to thin to desired consistency. Add the reserved asparagus tips. Stir in the yogurt and add cayenne pepper to taste. Serve immediately. Do not boil after adding the yogurt or the mixture will curdle. Serves 6.

Approximate nutritional analysis per serving:
Calories 133, Protein 10 g, Carbohydrates 13 g, Fat 5 g, Cholesterol 12 mg, Sodium 621 mg

YOGURT-CARROT SOUP

¼ cup (60 ml) butter
1 onion, chopped
2 cloves garlic, minced
½ tsp (3 ml) mustard seeds
½ tsp (3 ml) ground turmeric
½ tsp (3 ml) ground ginger
¼ tsp (1 ml) cayenne pepper
½ tsp (3 ml) salt
½ tsp (3 ml) ground cinnamon
½ tsp (3 ml) ground cumin
1 lb (455 g) carrots, peeled and thinly sliced
1 tbsp (15 ml) lemon juice
3½ cups (840 ml) water
2 cups (480 ml) nonfat plain yogurt
1 tbsp (15 ml) honey
black pepper, optional
fresh parsley, chopped, for garnish

Melt the butter in a skillet and sauté the onion and garlic until they are golden. Add the mustard seeds, turmeric, ginger, cayenne pepper, salt, cinnamon and cumin and sauté for several minutes, stirring constantly. Add the carrots and lemon juice, stir to combine and continue cooking for several more minutes. Add 2 cups of water. Cover and simmer for at least ½ hour or until the carrots are tender.

Purée the carrot mixture in a blender with the remaining 1½ cups of water. Pour the purée into a soup pot and stir in the yogurt with a whisk. Add the honey and heat the soup gently. Do not boil after adding the yogurt or the soup will curdle. Sprinkle with black pepper. Serve hot, garnished with parsley. Serves 4.

Approximate nutritional analysis per serving:
Calories 253, Protein 9 g, Carbohydrates 29 g, Fat 12 g, Cholesterol 33 mg, Sodium 519 mg

HEARTY CLAM CHOWDER

5 medium potatoes, pared and cut into ½-inch cubes
¾ cup (180 ml) chopped green onion, including tops
½ cup (120 ml) diced celery
1 carrot, thinly sliced
¼ cup diced red or green pepper
1 tsp (5 ml) minced garlic
2 cups (480 ml) water
2 tbsp (30 ml) margarine
1 tsp (5 ml) salt
1 tsp (5 ml) Worcestershire sauce
dash hot pepper sauce
2 6½-oz cans (390 g) minced clams
½ cup (120 ml) flour
2 cups (480 ml) unsweetened soy milk

Place potatoes, green onion, celery, carrot, pepper and garlic in large pan. Mix in water, margarine, salt, Worcestershire sauce and hot pepper sauce. Bring to boil, cover and cook 15 minutes over medium heat or until potatoes are tender. Drain clams, reserving liquid and adding water, if necessary, to make 1 cup. Combine clam liquid with flour and stir to make smooth paste. Pour flour paste into vegetables and cook, stirring, until mixture thickens. Add clams and soy milk. Continue cooking until chowder is hot, but do not boil. Serves 9.

Approximate nutritional analysis per serving:
Calories 180, Protein 10 g, Carbohydrates 28 g, Fat 4 g, Cholesterol 15 mg, Sodium 370 mg

BLACK-EYED PEA SOUP

11-oz pkg (330 g) black-eyed peas, cooked, with cooking liquid
2 tbsp (30 ml) cooking oil
1 cup (240 ml) minced celery
3 leeks, sliced, white part only
2 cloves garlic, minced
4 cups (960 ml) beef broth
1 bay leaf
2 tbsp (30 ml) chopped fresh thyme
*   or 1 tsp (5 ml) crushed dried thyme*
2 tbsp (30 ml) chopped fresh cilantro or parsley
1 tbsp (15 ml) chopped fresh marjoram
*   or 1 tsp (5 ml) crushed dried marjoram*
1 tbsp (15 ml) lemon juice
¼ tsp (1 ml) hot pepper sauce
bacon, cooked and crumbled, for garnish, optional
cilantro or parsley, snipped, for garnish, optional

Set cooked black-eyed peas aside; do not drain. In large saucepan or Dutch oven, heat oil; add celery, leeks and garlic. Sauté 5-8 minutes over medium heat. Stir in beef broth, bay leaf, thyme, cilantro, marjoram and lemon juice. Bring to boiling; reduce heat. Simmer, uncovered, 10 minutes. Remove bay leaf. Add peas and their liquid; process mixture in batches in food processor or blender. Return to pan; season to taste with salt and pepper and add hot pepper sauce. Reheat until warmed. Garnish each serving with crumbled bacon and cilantro or parsley. Serves 6 as main course.

Approximate nutritional analysis per serving:
Calories 274, Protein 15 g, Carbohydrates 43 g, Fat 6 g, Cholesterol 0 mg, Sodium 532 mg

FRENCH LENTIL SOUP

2 cups (480 ml) lentils
2 qts (1.9 l) water plus more as needed
2 onions, chopped
4 garlic cloves, minced
2 bay leaves
½ tsp (3 ml) ground cinnamon
½ tsp (3 ml) ground cloves
2 tsp (10 ml) ground cumin
2 cups (480 ml) chopped tomatoes or 1 cup (240 ml) puréed tomatoes
4 pepperoncini peppers, diced

Bring lentils and water to boil. Simmer 1 hour on very low heat. Add remaining ingredients. Add water as needed and simmer over very low flame 1 more hour. Add salt to taste. Serves 12.

Notes: Ordinary green lentils take longer to cook and have a less subtle flavor. This soup can be made in approximately 1 hour if cooked at higher temperatures, but lentils will lose their shape.

Approximate nutritional analysis per serving:
Calories 135, Protein 10 g, Carbohydrates 25 g, Fat .6 g, Cholesterol 0 mg, Sodium 8 mg

LEMONY LENTIL SOUP

3 cups (720 ml) water
1 cup (240 ml) dried brown, green or red lentils
1 large onion, finely chopped
3½ cups (840 ml) vegetable broth
3 tbsp (45 ml) extra-virgin olive oil
2 tsp (10 ml) minced garlic
1 lemon rind, freshly grated
½ cup (120 ml) fresh lemon juice

Bring water, lentils, onion, broth, oil and garlic to a boil in a 3-quart pot. Reduce heat, partially cover and simmer 30 minutes or until lentils are tender. Stir in lemon peel and juice. Serve promptly or refrigerate up to 3 days. Serves 4.

Approximate nutritional analysis per serving:
Calories 312, Protein 15 g, Carbohydrates 38 g, Fat 11 g, Cholesterol 0 mg, Sodium 322 mg

SPICY BLACK BEAN SOUP

2 tsp (10 ml) vegetable oil
1 onion, chopped
1 clove garlic, minced or pressed
2 14½-oz cans (870 g) diced tomatoes, undrained
3 15-oz cans (1.4 kg) black beans, drained, rinsed and puréed
1¾ cups (415 ml) vegetable or chicken broth
1 jalapeño chile, seeded and minced
2 tsp (10 ml) cumin seeds
¼ cup (60 ml) finely chopped green onion
shredded cheese, for garnish, optional
nonfat plain yogurt, for garnish, optional
cilantro leaves, for garnish, optional

In 4-6–quart saucepan, combine oil, onion and garlic. Cook over medium heat, stirring frequently, until onion is tender. Add tomatoes, beans, broth, chile and cumin seeds. Bring to boil; reduce heat and simmer, uncovered, about 10 minutes or until flavors are blended. Stir in green onion. Ladle into bowls; garnish as desired. Serves 8.

Approximate nutritional analysis per 1-cup serving:
Calories 261, Protein 17 g, Carbohydrates 44 g, Fat 2 g, Cholesterol 0 mg, Sodium 358 mg

GARBANZO SOUP

1 tbsp (15 ml) unrefined olive oil
½ cup (120 ml) chopped onion
4 cups (960 ml) cold water
½ cup (120 ml) garbanzo flour
2 tbsp (30 ml) soy sauce
1 tsp (5 ml) crushed sweet basil leaves
pinch garlic powder, optional

Preheat heavy saucepan, then add oil and onion and sauté until soft. Add 1 cup cold water. Stir in flour until smooth. Stir in remaining water gradually. Add seasonings. Let cook over medium-low heat until slightly thickened, stirring occasionally, or over higher heat, stirring constantly. Do not allow to boil. Serves 4.

Approximate nutritional analysis per serving:
Calories 106, Protein 4 g, Carbohydrates 13 g, Fat 5 g, Cholesterol 0 mg, Sodium 521 mg

ALMOST CHINESE HOT & SOUR SOUP

2 cups (480 ml) vegetable stock
2 cups (480 ml) plus 3 tbsp (45 ml) water
8 oz (240 g) hard tofu, slivered (2x¼x¼ inches)
2 cups (480 ml) slivered Napa cabbage
½ cup (120 ml) slivered fresh or reconstituted shiitake mushrooms
¼ cup (60 ml) coarsely grated carrots
1 tsp (5 ml) peeled and minced ginger
1 tbsp (15 ml) soy sauce
¾ tsp (4 ml) salt
2 tbsp (30 ml) white vinegar
⅛-¼ tsp (.5-1 ml) cayenne
2 tbsp (30 ml) cornstarch
cilantro, chopped scallions, garlic-chives or squeeze
 of fresh lemon, for garnish, optional

Boil stock and 2 cups water over medium-high heat. Add tofu, cabbage, mushrooms, carrots, ginger, soy sauce and salt. Return to boil, lower heat and simmer 4-5 minutes. Add vinegar and cayenne. Mix cornstarch and 3 tbsp water together. Add to soup and cook for 1-2 minutes. Garnish with any of the suggested items and serve very hot. Serves 6.

Approximate nutritional analysis per serving:
Calories 72, Protein 4 g, Carbohydrates 9 g, Fat 2 g, Cholesterol 0 mg, Sodium 569 mg

MINESTRONE SOUP

2 qts (1.9 l) vegetable broth
½ lb (230 g) dry kidney beans or lima beans
½ lb (230 g) fresh or frozen peas
1 small green cabbage, finely chopped
½ lb (230 g) fresh spinach leaves, shredded
4 carrots, finely chopped
4 stalks celery, finely chopped
1 yellow onion, finely chopped
4 garlic cloves, minced
½ cup (120 ml) raw brown rice
1 tbsp (15 ml) finely chopped fresh parsley
½ tsp (3 ml) sage
¼ cup (60 ml) extra-virgin olive oil, optional

Soak beans overnight. Put all ingredients in large stockpot. Bring to boil, stirring occasionally. Reduce heat and simmer until beans are tender. Salt and pepper to taste. This soup can be cooked in a crockpot for 8 hours on low. Serve with crusty French bread. Serves 10.

Approximate nutritional analysis per serving:
Calories 196, Protein 9 g, Carbohydrates 34 g, Fat .8 g, Cholesterol 0 mg, Sodium 407 mg

FRENCH ONION SOUP

1 bouquet garni (includes thyme, Italian parsley and bay leaf)
1 tbsp (15 ml) olive oil
4 cups (960 ml) sliced onions
2 tbsp (30 ml) sliced fresh garlic
4 cups (960 ml) low-sodium chicken broth
fresh ground black pepper
4 ½-inch-thick slices French bread
2 oz (60 g) reduced-fat Swiss cheese, grated

Finely chop the thyme leaves to equal 1-2 tsp; chop the Italian parsley and set aside.

Place the olive oil, onion, bay leaf and thyme in a nonstick saucepan and cook slowly until the onion turns light brown. This color is important as it indicates a rich, sweet flavor. Add the garlic and cook for 5 minutes. Add the chicken broth and simmer 20 minutes. Stir in the parsley and pepper to taste.

Divide the soup into four ovenproof bowls. Top each serving with French bread and ½ oz cheese. Brown under the broiler. Serve immediately. Serves 4.

Approximate nutritional analysis per serving:
Calories 290, Protein 11 g, Carbohydrates 27 g, Fat 7 g, Cholesterol 5 mg, Sodium 224 mg

GAZPACHO

2 14½-oz cans (870 g) diced tomatoes, undrained
14½-oz can (435 ml) vegetable or chicken broth
1 red onion, minced
1 green bell pepper, chopped
1 cucumber, peeled and chopped
1 stalk celery, chopped
1 clove garlic, minced
2 tbsp (30 ml) lemon juice
¼ tsp (1 ml) black pepper

In large bowl combine all ingredients. Cover and chill several hours. If desired, purée half of soup in blender or food processor and stir into remaining half. Serves 10.

Approximate nutritional analysis per serving:
Calories 37, Protein 2 g, Carbohydrates 6 g, Fat .3 g, Cholesterol 0 mg, Sodium 259 mg

CHICKEN-TORTILLA SOUP

4 cups (960 ml) low-sodium chicken broth
6 oz (180 g) boneless, skinless chicken breast, cut into ¼-inch strips
½ cup (120 ml) sliced onion
½ cup (120 ml) sliced red pepper
½ cup (120 ml) sliced Passilla chile or green pepper
1 cup (240 ml) diced Roma tomatoes
2 cloves fresh garlic, chopped
¼ tsp (1 ml) cumin
1 jalapeño or serrano chile, chopped and seeded, optional
2 tbsp (30 ml) chopped fresh oregano
2 tbsp (30 ml) chopped fresh cilantro, plus 4 sprigs, for garnish
12 corn tortilla chips

In a medium saucepan bring the chicken broth to a boil; add the chicken strips and cook for 5 minutes, skimming the top. Add the vegetables, cumin and chile and cook for 10 more minutes. Chop the oregano and cilantro, reserving four sprigs of cilantro for garnish. Add the fresh herbs at the last minute and serve, garnishing each bowl with a sprig of cilantro and 3 tortilla chips. Serves 4.

Approximate nutritional analysis per serving:
Calories 133, Protein 14 g, Carbohydrates 12 g, Fat 4 g, Cholesterol 23 mg, Sodium 132 mg

FAMILY GAZPACHO

1 qt (960 ml) tomato juice
1 cup (240 ml) chopped fresh tomatoes
1 cup (240 ml) chopped cucumber
½ cup (120 ml) chopped red onion
1 cup (240 ml) croutons
½ cup (120 ml) Italian parsley

Chill juice. Pour into five bowls; garnish with tomatoes, cucumber, onion, croutons and parsley. Serves 5.

Approximate nutritional analysis per serving:
Calories 100, Protein 3 g, Carbohydrates 21 g, Fat .6 g, Cholesterol 0 mg, Sodium 635 mg

PEA POD-SPINACH SOUP

3 cups (720 ml) chicken broth
3 cups (720 ml) vegetable broth or additional chicken broth
1 tbs (15 ml) soy sauce
pinch cayenne
2 oz (60 g) snow peas, stringed and halved crosswise
2 cups (480 ml) spinach leaves, torn and stems removed
1 cup (240 ml) tofu, drained and broken into chunks
½ cup (120 ml) enoki mushrooms
3 green onions, chopped
1 hard-cooked egg, chopped, optional

Heat broths in Dutch oven or 3-quart saucepan; add soy sauce and red pepper; simmer 2 minutes. Add snow peas, spinach leaves and tofu chunks. Cut off bottom ½ inch of enoki mushroom stems; add to soup with chopped onion. Simmer 1 minute. Serve soup in bowls, with some chopped egg sprinkled on top. Serves 6.

Approximate nutritional analysis per serving:
Calories 73, Protein 8 g, Carbohydrates 4 g, Fat 3 g, Cholesterol 0 mg, Sodium 828 mg

Salads

SOUTHWESTERN CHICKEN CAESAR SALAD

¼ cup (60 ml) chopped fresh cilantro
¼ cup (60 ml) green chile
1 cup (240 ml) low-sodium, low-fat Caesar salad dressing
8 cups (1.9 l) chopped romaine lettuce
4 4-oz (480 g) chicken breasts, grilled and cut into ½-inch strips
2 red peppers, lightly grilled and cut into 2-inch strips

Mix cilantro and chile into salad dressing. Add to lettuce and toss together gently. Place ¼ mixture in center of each of four large plates. Garnish salad with chicken and peppers and serve. Serves 4.

Approximate nutritional analysis per serving:
Calories 281, Protein 31 g, Carbohydrates 20 g, Fat 8 g, Cholesterol 75 mg, Sodium 100 mg

THAI CHICKEN NOODLE SALAD

DRESSING:
1 cup (240 ml) seasoned rice vinegar
1 tbsp (15 ml) chopped fresh garlic
1 tbsp (15 ml) chopped fresh ginger
5 tsp (25 ml) sesame oil
1 tbsp (25 ml) low-sodium soy sauce
¼ cup (60 ml) lime juice
6 tbsp (90 ml) mixed fresh herbs
¼ tsp (1 ml) white pepper

4 cups (960 ml) cooked egg noodles
12 oz (360 g) cooked boneless, skinless chicken breast
1 cup (240 ml) bean sprouts
½ cup (120 ml) shredded raw carrots
½ cup (120 ml) blanched snow peas
2 cups (480 ml) chopped iceberg lettuce
½ cup (120 ml) chopped red bell pepper, plus additional, for garnish
¼ cup (60 ml) peanuts, dry roasted and unsalted
herb leaves, for garnish

Dressing: Mix all ingredients together. Yields 1½ cups.

    Place all salad ingredients in a large bowl and toss with dressing. Serve in large bowls and garnish with chopped red pepper and herb leaves. Serves 4.

Approximate nutritional analysis per serving w/dressing:
Calories 480, Protein 33 g, Carbohydrates 54 g, Fat 16 g, Cholesterol 99 mg, Sodium 320 mg

SESAME CHICKEN SALAD

DRESSING:
¼ cup (60 ml) chicken broth
1 tbsp (15 ml) peanut oil
3 tbsp (45 ml) white wine vinegar
3 tbsp (45 ml) soy sauce
1 tsp (5 ml) sesame oil

3 cups (720 ml) cooked long-grain rice
2 cups (480 ml) sliced cooked chicken breast
¼ lb (115 g) snow peas, sliced into strips
1 medium cucumber, cut into strips
1 medium red pepper, cut into strips
½ cup (120 ml) sliced green onion
2 tbsp (30 ml) toasted sesame seeds

Dressing: Combine all ingredients in jar; cover tightly and shake vigorously. Yields ¾ cup.
Combine all salad ingredients; stir well. Toss with dressing. Serve at room temperature or slightly chilled. Serves 6.

Approximate nutritional analysis per serving w/dressing:
Calories 328, Protein 34 g, Carbohydrates 28 g, Fat 8 g, Cholesterol 80 mg, Sodium 623 mg

WRANGLER STEAK & PASTA SALAD

12 oz (360 g) uncooked rotelli or rotini pasta
1 lb (455 g) chuck blade steak, broiled and cut into bite-size cubes
15-oz can (450 g) pinto beans, rinsed and drained
15-oz can (450 g) red kidney beans, rinsed and drained
1 cup (240 ml) chopped red onion
1 cup (240 ml) chopped green bell pepper
1½ cups (355 ml) prepared barbecue sauce
½ cup (120 ml) cider vinegar
2 tsp (10 ml) dry mustard
½ tsp (3 ml) ground black pepper

Cook and drain pasta. In large salad bowl combine steak cubes, pasta, pinto and kidney beans, onion and bell pepper; set aside. In medium bowl combine barbecue sauce, vinegar, dry mustard and black pepper, blending well. Pour over pasta salad; toss well to coat. Serves 8.

Approximate nutritional analysis per serving:
Calories 369, Protein 21 g, Carbohydrates 62 g, Fat 4 g, Cholesterol 25 mg, Sodium 942 mg

THAI STEAK & RICE SALAD

DRESSING:
½ cup (120 ml) seasoned rice wine vinegar
3 tbsp (45 ml) olive oil
2 tbsp (30 ml) soy sauce
1 tsp (5 ml) garlic powder
½ tsp (3 ml) ground ginger
½ tsp (3 ml) ground black pepper
2 tbsp (30 ml) chopped fresh cilantro leaves

1 lb (455 g) chuck blade or top sirloin steak,
    grilled or broiled and cut into 2-inch slices
1 cup (240 ml) long-grain rice, cooked and cooled
½ cup (120 ml) chopped red bell pepper
¼ cup (60 ml) thinly sliced green onion
¼ cup (60 ml) shredded carrots
1 tbsp (15 ml) toasted sesame seeds

In small bowl combine dressing ingredients; set aside. In large bowl combine steak and salad ingredients. Pour on dressing and toss to coat. Serves 4.

Approximate nutritional analysis per serving:
Calories 444, Protein 27 g, Carbohydrates 44 g, Fat 18 g, Cholesterol 50 mg, Sodium 526 mg

GRILLED CHILE-SHRIMP SALAD

½ lb (230 g) large raw shrimp, shelled and deveined, or scallops
½ cup (120 ml) water
¼ cup (60 ml) lime juice
1 tsp (5 ml) sesame oil or vegetable oil
2 tbsp (30 ml) minced green onion
2 tbsp (30 ml) minced fresh cilantro
1 dried habañero chile, rehydrated and very finely minced
1 clove garlic, minced
2 cups (480 ml) shredded green or yellow zucchini
2 cups (480 ml) shredded carrots

Place shrimp or scallops in nonmetal dish. Stir together water, lime juice, oil, onion, cilantro, chile and garlic; pour over shrimp. Cover and chill for 2-6 hours.

To serve preheat broiler or barbecue grill. Place shredded zucchini and carrot in steamer over simmering water. Cover and steam about 3-5 minutes or until tender. Drain shrimp; thread on skewers. Broil or grill 3-5 minutes or until pink and opaque. Serve shrimp over steamed vegetables. Serves 4.

Approximate nutritional analysis per serving:
Calories 104, Protein 13 g, Carbohydrates 9 g, Fat 2 g, Cholesterol 111 mg, Sodium 151 mg

ITALIAN BEAN & PASTA SALAD

2 cups (480 ml) anasazi beans, cooked
2 cups (480 ml) cooked spinach noodles or vegetable rotelli
½ cup (120 ml) chopped onion
1 medium tomato, chopped
¼ cup (60 ml) chopped bell pepper
1 tbsp (15 ml) sesame seeds
2 tbsp (30 ml) unrefined olive oil
2 tbsp (30 ml) lemon juice
1 tsp (5 ml) garlic powder
¼ tsp (1 ml) oregano
¼ tsp (1 ml) basil
¼ tsp (1 ml) thyme
¼ tsp (1 ml) sea salt, optional

Gently mix all ingredients in a large mixing bowl. Refrigerate until cold and serve. Allowing the mixture to set for 1 hour before serving will enhance the flavor. Serves 4.

Approximate nutritional analysis per serving:
Calories 297, Protein 11 g, Carbohydrates 44 g, Fat 9 g, Cholesterol 0 mg, Sodium 16 mg

PRIMAVERA PASTA SALAD

1½ tbsp (25 ml) olive oil
1½ tbsp (25 ml) butter or margarine
1½ cups (355 ml) broccoli florets
2 cloves garlic, minced
2 medium tomatoes, seeded and diced
¾ cup (180 ml) julienned zucchini
½ cup (120 ml) julienned carrots
¼ cup (60 ml) honey
¼ cup (60 ml) lemon juice
1½ tsp (8 ml) grated lemon peel
¾ tsp (4 ml) crushed dried basil
¾ tsp (4 ml) crushed dried oregano
6 oz (180 g) linguine or fettuccine noodles, cooked
Parmesan cheese, grated

Heat oil and butter in large skillet over medium-high heat; add broccoli and garlic and stir-fry 2 minutes. Reduce heat to low and add tomatoes, zucchini, carrot, honey, lemon juice, lemon peel and seasonings. Salt and pepper to taste. Simmer about 4 minutes or until vegetables are tender, stirring gently. Toss with noodles; cool. Sprinkle with Parmesan cheese. Serve at room temperature or chilled. Serves 6.

Approximate nutritional analysis per serving:
Calories 165, Protein 3 g, Carbohydrates 26 g, Fat 7 g, Cholesterol 8 mg, Sodium 44 mg

KASHA & BLACK BEAN COMBO

2 cups (480 ml) kasha, whole or coarse
4 cups (960 ml) chicken or vegetable broth
8 oz (240 g) white cheddar or Monterey Jack cheese,
    cut into ¼-inch cubes
15-oz can (450 g) black beans, drained and rinsed
½ cup (120 ml) thinly sliced celery
½ cup (120 ml) diced sweet red pepper
¼ cup (60 ml) diced green pepper
¼ cup (60 ml) sliced red onion
¼ cup (60 ml) chopped fresh basil
½ cup (120 ml) Dijon vinaigrette
2 cups (480 ml) fresh spinach, cut into strips,
    plus additional leaves, for garnish
4 slices bacon, fried crisp and crumbled

Prepare kasha using broth. In large nonmetal bowl combine kasha, cheese, black beans, celery, peppers, onion and basil. Mix well, then add vinaigrette and toss. Cover and chill for at least 2 hours. Before serving, add spinach; toss. Arrange additional spinach leaves in salad bowl or on platter. Top with salad and sprinkle with bacon. Serves 5.

Approximate nutritional analysis per serving:
Calories 463, Protein 25 g, Carbohydrates 46 g, Fat 22 g, Cholesterol 53 mg, Sodium 587 mg

MARINATED PASTA SALAD

1 lb (455 g) uncooked pasta shells
⅓ cup (80 ml) extra-virgin olive oil
⅓ cup (80 ml) red wine vinegar
1 tsp (5 ml) basil-flavored oil
1 large green bell pepper, minced
1 small red onion, minced
1 cup (240 ml) pimiento, drained and minced
½ cup (120 ml) minced fresh parsley
fresh black pepper
½ tsp (3 ml) salt, optional
small cubes mozzarella cheese, optional
handful toasted pine nuts, optional

Cook the shells until al dente, 5-8 minutes at the most. Drain the cooked shells in a colander, rinse under tepid water and shake to drain thoroughly. Transfer the warm shells to a bowl and immediately toss with the olive oil. Cover and chill at least 30 minutes. Add the remaining ingredients and mix well. Serve very cold. Serves 8.

Approximate nutritional analysis per serving:
Calories 265, Protein 6 g, Carbohydrates 37 g, Fat 11 g, Cholesterol 0 mg, Sodium 8 mg

SPRING GINGER SALAD

SALAD:
4 cups (960 ml) sliced bok choy, stem and leaves
2 tangerines, peeled and halved
2 large carrots, sliced diagonally
4 oz (120 g) bamboo shoots, rinsed and drained
4 tbsp (60 ml) seasoned rice vinegar
1 tsp (5 ml) sesame oil
1 tsp (5 ml) minced garlic
2 tbsp (30 ml) chopped fresh gingerroot
1 tsp (5 ml) fresh ground pepper

TOFU:
10½-oz pkg firm tofu, sliced and cubed
1 tsp (5 ml) sesame oil

Mix salad ingredients and marinate overnight to 2 days.

Sauté tofu in hot oil in nonstick wok or nonstick skillet. Cook about 8-10 minutes or until dark golden color on both sides. Cool on paper towel. Drain off excess liquid from salad. Add tofu to vegetables and serve. Serves 6.

Approximate nutritional analysis per 1-cup serving:
Calories 109, Protein 7 g, Carbohydrates 16 g, Fat 3 g, Cholesterol 0 mg, Sodium 99 mg

MARINATED GREEN BEAN & RED PEPPER SALAD

2 small red bell peppers
12 oz (360 g) green beans, blanched
½ of 10½-oz pkg (158 g) light tofu, cubed
1 green onion, thinly sliced
3 tbsp (45 ml) chopped parsley
⅓ cup (80 ml) extra-virgin olive oil
⅓ cup (80 ml) lemon juice
1 clove garlic, minced
½ tsp (3 ml) salt substitute
¼ tsp (1 ml) coarsely ground black pepper
½ tsp (3 ml) dry mustard
½ tsp (3 ml) oregano
½ tsp (3 ml) cumin

Roast bell peppers in broiler until skin is charred on all sides. Place in plastic bag and let cool. Remove skin and seeds. Cut in thin strips.

In mixing bowl combine pepper strips, green beans, tofu, green onion and parsley. In small mixing bowl combine olive oil, lemon juice, garlic, salt substitute, black pepper, mustard, oregano and cumin. Blend well.

Toss olive oil and seasonings with green bean mixture. Cover and refrigerate several hours to develop flavor. Serves 4.

Approximate nutritional analysis per serving:
Calories 149, Protein 4 g, Carbohydrates 10 g, Fat 10 g, Cholesterol 0 mg, Sodium 23 mg

JASMINE RICE SALAD

6 cups (1.4 l) cooked jasmine rice

SAUCE:
3 cups (720 ml) water
3 stalks fresh lemon grass or 2 tbsp (30 ml) dried lemon grass
¼ cup (60 ml) soy sauce
1 cup (240 ml) sugar or ¾ cup (180 ml) honey
2 tbsp (30 ml) grated fresh ginger or ½ tsp (3 ml) dried ginger
⅓ tsp (2 ml) cayenne or hot chile powder
juice and grated peel of 2 limes

1½ cups (355 ml) shredded coconut
1 cup (240 ml) finely chopped spinach
1 cucumber, thinly sliced and quartered
1 cup (240 ml) jicama, diced into ½-inch pieces
¼ red bell pepper, cut into 1-inch strips
½ cup (120 ml) chopped green onion
½ cup (120 ml) snow peas
1 cup (240 ml) bean sprouts
1 cup (240 ml) diced peeled orange
½ cup (120 ml) chopped cilantro
1 cup (240 ml) chopped roasted peanuts, for garnish

First boil the rice according to package directions. Cool. To quickly cool the rice spread it in a thin layer on cookie sheets or in a large bowl.

In a saucepan combine the water and lemon grass and simmer for at least 8 minutes to make lemon grass tea. Then set aside to cool. Strain the lemon grass from the tea. To the tea add the rest of the sauce ingredients and mix or blend well.

In a frying pan dry-roast the coconut by stirring it over medium heat until toasted golden. Set aside to cool.

Assemble the salad by gently tossing the rice, coconut and vegetables with the sauce. Serve chilled. Garnish with the peanuts when serving. Serves 8.

Approximate nutritional analysis per serving:
Calories 437, Protein 10 g, Carbohydrates 72 g, Fat 14 g, Cholesterol 0 mg, Sodium 527 mg

ASIAN RICE-VEGETABLE SALAD

½ cup (120 ml) cauliflower florets
½ cup (120 ml) broccoli florets
½ cup (120 ml) carrots, cut into ½-inch slices
½ cup (120 ml) snow peas
½ cup (120 ml) onions, cut into ½-inch cubes
2 tbsp (30 ml) soy sauce
2½ cups (590 ml) cooked brown rice
1 tsp (5 ml) cider vinegar
dash ginger
dash lemon juice

Place the vegetables in a heavy saucepan with the soy sauce. Cover and simmer over low heat for 5-7 minutes until the vegetables are barely tender. Set aside to cool and add the remaining ingredients. Chill before serving. Serves 4.

Approximate nutritional analysis per serving:
Calories 159, Protein 5 g, Carbohydrates 33 g, Fat 1 g, Cholesterol 0 mg, Sodium 528 mg

BROWN BASMATI RICE SALAD

DRESSING:
⅔ cup (160 ml) plain yogurt
2 tbsp (30 ml) lemon juice
1 small clove garlic, minced or pressed
¼ tsp (1 ml) salt
1½ tsp (8 ml) dill weed

⅓ cup (80 ml) chopped black olives
½ cup (120 ml) chopped fresh parsley
¼ cup (60 ml) chopped celery
¼ cup (60 ml) chopped red pepper
2 green onions, chopped
1 large tomato, chopped
½ cup (120 ml) fresh peas
2 cups (480 ml) cooked and cooled brown basmati rice

Prepare dressing and let stand while chopping vegetables. Mix vegetables with rice, add dressing and toss. Serves 5.

Approximate nutritional analysis per 1-cup serving:
Calories 119, Protein 5 g, Carbohydrates 22 g, Fat 2 g, Cholesterol .6 mg, Sodium 223 mg

SESAME PASTA SALAD

12 oz (360 g) angel hair pasta
¼ cup (60 ml) Chinese sesame oil
4 tbsp (60 ml) soy sauce
½ cup (120 ml) minced watercress
½-1 tsp (3-5 ml) minced garlic
1 tsp (5 ml) hot chile oil

Cook pasta to al dente stage, drain and toss with remaining ingredients. Add sea salt and fresh ground pepper to taste. Chill salad for several hours before serving. Serves 6.

Approximate nutritional analysis per serving:
Calories 302, Protein 8 g, Carbohydrates 49 g, Fat 11 g, Cholesterol 0 mg, Sodium 687 mg

SPICY CUCUMBER-ORANGE SALAD

1 cucumber, thinly sliced
1 large orange, peeled, thinly sliced and cut in quarters
½ red onion, thinly sliced and separated into rings
1 large fresh Anaheim chile, seeded and chopped
1 cup (240 ml) white vinegar
⅓ cup (80 ml) salad oil
1 tbsp (15 ml) chopped fresh oregano or 1 tsp (5 ml) dried oregano
2 tsp (10 ml) chopped fresh sage or ½ tsp (3 ml) dried sage
1 tbsp (15 ml) chopped fresh cilantro
½ tsp (3 ml) salt
1 tsp (5 ml) ground black pepper

In a deep glass bowl toss together the cucumber slices, orange pieces, onion and chile.

In a covered container place the vinegar, oil and remaining ingredients; shake together until blended. Pour over salad mixture; stir to coat all ingredients. Cover and chill 3 hours or overnight, stirring occasionally. Serve with a slotted spoon as a side-dish salad or relish. The marinade can be saved and used for salad dressing. Serves 3.

Approximate nutritional analysis per serving w/ 1 tbsp marinade:
Calories 71, Protein 1 g, Carbohydrates 10 g, Fat 4 g, Cholesterol 0 mg, Sodium 52 mg

JICAMA, ORANGE & ONION SALAD

2 cups (480 ml) torn lettuce leaves
2 navel oranges, peeled and thinly sliced
4 thin slices red onion
1 cup (240 ml) peeled and julienned jicama

DRESSING:
⅓ cup (80 ml) orange juice
½ tsp (3 ml) light olive oil or vegetable oil
1 tbsp (15 ml) finely chopped fresh cilantro
⅛-¼ tsp (.5-1 ml) chili powder

In large salad bowl place torn lettuce. Cut orange slices into quarters; toss into lettuce with onion and jicama. For dressing shake together all ingredients in shaker jar; toss with salad. Serves 4.

Approximate nutritional analysis per serving w/ dressing:
Calories 66, Protein 2 g, Carbohydrates 14 g, Fat .8 g, Cholesterol 0 mg, Sodium 6 mg

NEW CAESAR-STYLE SALAD

3 ½-inch-thick slices French bread, cubed
¼ cup (60 ml) lemon juice
1 tsp (5 ml) olive or vegetable oil
1 tsp (5 ml) anchovy paste
1 clove elephant garlic, peeled and finely minced
¼ tsp (1 ml) pepper
3 cups (720 ml) torn limestone lettuce
3 cups (720 ml) torn romaine lettuce
2 tbsp (30 ml) grated Parmesan cheese

Sprinkle bread cubes on baking sheet; bake in 350°F (180°C) oven for 10-12 minutes or until toasted. Meanwhile in small bowl stir together lemon juice, oil, anchovy paste, garlic and pepper. Remove toasted bread from oven; place in shallow bowl. Sprinkle 2 tbsp of dressing mixture over croutons; toss to coat.

In salad bowl toss together limestone and romaine lettuce. Add croutons, remaining dressing and Parmesan cheese; toss well. Serves 4.

Approximate nutritional analysis per serving:
Calories 92, Protein 4 g, Carbohydrates 14 g, Fat 2 g, Cholesterol 3 mg, Sodium 177 mg

ARUGULA & TOMATO SALAD

4 vine-ripened tomatoes
1 red onion
2 bunches fresh arugula
2 cups (480 ml) canned cannellini or red kidney beans,
    rinsed and drained
2 tbsp (30 ml) extra-virgin olive oil
1 clove fresh garlic, chopped
1 tbsp (15 ml) balsamic vinegar
fresh ground black pepper

Slice the tomatoes and red onion in rings and place in alternate layers with the arugula and ½ cup beans on each of four plates.

Mix the oil, garlic and vinegar and spoon over the salad. Finish with fresh ground pepper. Serves 4.

Approximate nutritional analysis per serving:
Calories 224, Protein 10 g, Carbohydrates 32 g, Fat 8 g, Cholesterol 0 mg, Sodium 225 mg

MIXED VEGETABLE SLAW

½ medium green cabbage
½ medium red cabbage
¼ medium red onion
1 large carrot
1 small beet
½ small red bell pepper

DRESSING:
¼-½ cup (60-120 ml) green goddess dressing
2 tbsp (30 ml) balsamic vinegar
1 clove garlic, pressed
1 tbsp (25 ml) dill weed or 3 tbsp (45 ml) chopped fresh dill
1 tbsp (15 ml) soy sauce

Grate vegetables using food processor or by hand. Mix dressing ingredients well and stir into grated vegetables. Serves 4.

Approximate nutritional analysis per serving:
Calories 109, Protein 2 g, Carbohydrates 11 g, Fat 7 g, Cholesterol 0 mg, Sodium 457 mg

CHILLED DILLED CARROT SALAD

2 cups (480 ml) thinly sliced carrots
½ cup (120 ml) diced shallots or red onion
1 tbsp (15 ml) olive oil
1 tbsp (15 ml) red wine vinegar
2-3 tbsp (30-45 ml) chopped fresh dill

Parboil carrots until tender yet crisp, about 2 minutes. Rinse under cold water and drain. Combine carrots and shallots. Mix remaining ingredients in small bowl until well blended, adding salt and pepper to taste. Pour over carrot mixture and toss well. Refrigerate at least 3 hours to blend flavors. Serves 4.

Approximate nutritional analysis per serving:
Calories 46, Protein 1 g, Carbohydrates 9 g, Fat 1 g, Cholesterol 0 mg, Sodium 157 mg

ENSALADA DE TOMATILLO

½ cup (120 ml) salad oil
¼ cup (60 ml) white vinegar
3 sprigs cilantro, chopped
½ jalapeño chile, seeded and chopped
1 clove garlic, minced
1½ tsp (8 ml) chopped fresh oregano
*   or ½ tsp (3 ml) crushed dried oregano*
1½ tsp (8 ml) chopped fresh basil or ½ tsp (3 ml) crushed dried basil
shredded lettuce
2 cups (480 ml) zucchini cut into ½-inch chunks
2 red tomatoes, cut into wedges
4 tomatillos, peeled, washed and chopped
green onion, sliced

Prepare the dressing in a lidded jar by combining the salad oil, vinegar, cilantro, chile, garlic, oregano and basil. Cover and shake well to blend.

Arrange a bed of shredded lettuce on each of four salad plates. Top each salad with some of the zucchini, tomato and tomatillo. Sprinkle with the onion. Shake the dressing again; drizzle it over the salads. Serves 4.

Approximate nutritional analysis per serving w/ 1 tbsp dressing:
Calories 154, Protein 2 g, Carbohydrates 7 g, Fat 2 g, Cholesterol 0 mg, Sodium 115 mg

DILLED POTATO SALAD

16 oz (480 g) red skin potatoes
1 cup (240 ml) nonfat plain yogurt
¼ cup (60 ml) whole grain mustard
¼ cup (60 ml) seasoned rice vinegar
½ cup (120 ml) diced red onion
½ cup (120 ml) diced celery
fresh ground pepper
4 tbsp (60 ml) chopped fresh dill plus 4 sprigs, for garnish

Boil the potatoes in lightly salted water until tender. Set aside to cool. Cut the potatoes into quarters. Mix the yogurt and the rest of the ingredients together. Add the potatoes. Chill. Garnish with sprigs of dill. Serves 4.

Approximate nutritional analysis per serving:
Calories 181, Protein 7 g, Carbohydrates 37 g, Fat 1 g, Cholesterol 1 mg, Sodium 258 mg

DRIED TOMATO-POTATO SALAD

1 lb (455 g) baby red or baby white potatoes, quartered and cooked
3-oz pkg (90 g) dried tomatoes, reconstituted
1 leek, trimmed and thinly sliced, white part only
⅓ cup (80 ml) light sour cream
2 tbsp (30 ml) skim milk
2 tbsp (30 ml) chopped fresh basil or 2 tsp (10 ml) dried basil
1 tbsp (15 ml) chopped fresh dill or 1 tsp (5 ml) dill weed
1 clove garlic, minced

Place potatoes in large bowl. Sliver dried tomatoes; reserve ½ cup of tomatoes for dressing. Add remaining tomatoes to potatoes and leeks. Toss gently.

In food processor or blender place reserved tomatoes, sour cream, milk, basil, dill, garlic and salt and pepper to taste. Cover and process until smooth. Spoon onto salad; toss gently to coat. Serves 5.

Approximate nutritional analysis per serving:
Calories 162, Protein 5 g, Carbohydrates 32 g, Fat 3 g, Cholesterol 6 mg, Sodium 375 mg

Rice & Grains

99 LBS. NET WEIGHT

WHOLE BEAN
UNCOATED

TABLE RICE

ITALIAN PISTACHIO PILAF

3½ cups (840 ml) water
1 cup (240 ml) white basmati rice, uncooked
2½ tsp (13 ml) salt, optional
1 cup (240 ml) diced onion
1 cup (240 ml) diced red bell pepper
2 tbsp (30 ml) chopped fresh garlic
2 cups (480 ml) flaked seitan, thinly sliced at 45° angle
3 tbsp (45 ml) ground fennel
1 tsp (5 ml) ground black pepper
3 tbsp (45 ml) olive oil
1 cup (240 ml) sliced scallions
1 cup (240 ml) chopped pistachios

Bring water to simmer. Add rice and ½ tsp of salt and simmer for 10 minutes. Cover pot and turn off heat. Let sit until cooked, about 5 minutes.

Sauté onion, bell pepper, garlic, seitan, fennel, black pepper and remaining 2 tsp salt in olive oil until vegetables are soft, about 10 minutes on medium heat. Add rice, scallions and pistachios. Serve hot with vegetable as light meal. Serves 8.

Approximate nutritional analysis per serving:
Calories 404, Protein 28 g, Carbohydrates 43 g, Fat 14 g, Cholesterol 0 mg, Sodium 25 mg

GOLDEN RICE CASSEROLE

juice of 1 lemon
2 cups (480 ml) white basmati rice, cooked
½ tsp (3 ml) turmeric
2 cups (480 ml) steamed vegetables, any combination of peas, onions,
*   broccoli, cauliflower, zucchini, carrots or mushrooms*
8 oz (240 g) nonfat plain yogurt
½ cup (120 ml) toasted cashews, whole or in pieces
½ cup (120 ml) raisins

Preheat the oven to 350°F (180°C). Combine the lemon juice, rice and turmeric. Spread half the rice in a buttered casserole dish. Layer with half the vegetables, then follow with half the yogurt, cashews and raisins. Repeat and place in oven for about 30 minutes or until heated through. Serve piping hot; if desired, add butter, margarine or shoyu sauce. Serves 12.

Approximate nutritional analysis per serving:
Calories 190, Protein 5 g, Carbohydrates 37 g, Fat 3 g, Cholesterol .3 mg, Sodium 57 mg

GREEN LEAF BROWN RICE WITH GARLIC CHIVES

1 cup (240 ml) sliced baby leeks and/or scallions
1-2 tbsp (15-30 ml) canola oil
1 cup (240 ml) brown rice, uncooked
2 cups (480 ml) water
2 tbsp (30 ml) garlic chives
2 tbsp (30 ml) chopped thyme

Lightly sauté leeks in canola oil until translucent. Add brown rice, sea salt to taste and water. Season with black pepper to taste, bring to boil and simmer about 45 minutes. When rice is cooked and fluffed, add garlic chives and chopped thyme. Serve with yogurt. Serves 6.

Approximate nutritional analysis per serving w/o yogurt:
Calories 202, Protein 4 g, Carbohydrates 40 g, Fat 4 g, Cholesterol 0 mg, Sodium 26 mg

SPANISH SHORT GRAIN

1 tbsp (15 ml) olive oil
1 bell pepper, chopped
1 large onion, chopped
2 cloves garlic, minced
1½ cups (355 ml) short-grain brown rice, uncooked
water
14½-oz can (435 g) chopped tomatoes, strained, with juice reserved
pinch cayenne, optional

Heat oil in 4-qt, thick-walled skillet or saucepan with tight-fitting lid. Sauté bell pepper, onion and garlic in oil briefly. Add rice and stir. Add water and juice from canned tomatoes to equal 3 cups. Bring to boil, reduce heat to low, cover and simmer for 30 minutes. Add tomatoes and cayenne, if desired, cover and continue cooking for another 15 minutes. Serve warm. Serves 6.

Approximate nutritional analysis per serving:
Calories 222, Protein 5 g, Carbohydrates 43 g, Fat 4 g, Cholesterol 0 mg, Sodium 11 mg

BASMATI RICE PILAF

¾ cup (180 g) basmati rice, uncooked
2 cups (480 ml) water
⅓ cup (80 ml) light or dark raisins
⅓ cup (80 ml) sliced green onion
1 tsp (5 ml) grated fresh ginger
¼ tsp (1 ml) ground cinnamon
pinch ground cloves or cardamom
½ cup (120 ml) pignolias or slivered almonds

In 2-quart saucepan combine rice, water, raisins, onion, ginger, cinnamon and cloves. Bring to boiling; reduce heat. Simmer, covered, for 20-30 minutes or until rice is tender. Stir in pignolias. Serves 6.

Approximate nutritional analysis per serving:
Calories 222, Protein 6 g, Carbohydrates 37 g, Fat 8 g, Cholesterol 0 mg, Sodium 3 mg

WILD MAJUDRA

1 cup (240 ml) wild rice, uncooked
3 cups (720 ml) water
½ cup (120 ml) lentils
1 onion, sliced in rings
¼ cup (60 ml) olive oil
1 red bell pepper, sliced
6 large mushrooms, sliced
½ cup (20 ml) cilantro leaves, chopped

Rinse rice and add to water in saucepan. Bring to boil, reduce heat and simmer for 15 minutes. Add lentils to rice and continue cooking for about 40-45 minutes, until rice grains have popped open and lentils are tender. In large skillet sauté onion in olive oil for 15 minutes. Add bell pepper and mushrooms and continue cooking for 10 more minutes. Add rice-lentil mixture to vegetables and cook briefly on high heat to absorb vegetable juices. Add cilantro, salt to taste and serve. Serves 6.

Approximate nutritional analysis per serving:
Calories 290, Protein 11 g, Carbohydrates 42 g, Fat 10 g, Cholesterol 0 mg, Sodium 8 mg

CURRIED WHOLE WHEAT COUSCOUS PILAF

1 small onion, chopped
1 clove garlic, minced
2 tbsp (30 ml) butter
1 cup (240 ml) sliced mushrooms
½ red bell pepper, chopped
½ cup (120 ml) fresh or frozen peas
½ cup (120 ml) chopped green onion
1½ cups (355 ml) water or broth
¼ tsp (1 ml) salt
2 tsp (10 ml) curry powder
1 cup (240 ml) whole wheat couscous

In covered saucepan on low heat sauté onion and garlic in butter until soft. Add mushrooms, bell pepper, peas and green onion and cook until nearly tender. Add water, salt and curry powder and bring to boil. Add couscous, stir, reduce heat, cover and cook for 3-5 minutes or until liquid is absorbed. Serves 8.

Approximate nutritional analysis per ½-cup serving:
Calories 184, Protein 6 g, Carbohydrates 33 g, Fat 3 g, Cholesterol 8 mg, Sodium 105 mg

KASHA VARNISHKAS

2 tbsp (30 ml) butter or margarine
½ cup (120 ml) chopped onion
½ cup (120 ml) sliced mushrooms
1 cup (240 ml) uncooked kasha
chicken or beef broth
2 tbsp (30 ml) minced fresh parsley
1 cup (240 ml) pasta bow knots (varnishkas)
2 tsp (10 ml) butter
minced parsley

In large skillet melt butter and sauté onion and mushrooms. Prepare kasha according to basic directions on package, using chicken or beef broth as liquid. Add sautéed vegetables when liquid is added and eliminate any additional butter or margarine.

While kasha is simmering, cook pasta in boiling salted water until just tender, about 12 minutes. Drain pasta, return to pan and add butter. Combine with kasha and sprinkle with parsley before serving. Serves 4.

Approximate nutritional analysis per serving:
Calories 300, Protein 9 g, Carbohydrates 46 g, Fat 10 g, Cholesterol 21 mg, Sodium 89 mg

KNISHES

PASTRY:
2 cups (480 ml) all-purpose flour
½ tsp (3 ml) salt
1 egg or 2 egg whites, plus 1 egg white, slightly beaten
2 tbsp (30 ml) vegetable oil, plus additional, for brushing dough
½ cup (120 ml) water

ONION FILLING:
1 cup (240 ml) chopped onion
2 tbsp (30 ml) butter or margarine
¾ cup (180 ml) cooked kasha
pinch pepper

CHICKEN FILLING:
1 cup (240 ml) diced cooked chicken
¾ cup (180 ml) cooked kasha
¼ cup (60 ml) finely chopped celery
3 tbsp (45 ml) mayonnaise
½ tsp (3 ml) poultry seasoning
½ tsp (3 ml) lemon juice
pinch salt

EGG FILLING:
¾ cup (180 ml) cooked kasha
3 hard-cooked eggs, chopped
3 tbsp (45 ml) pickle relish
1 tbsp (15 ml) minced onion
2 tsp (10 ml) prepared mustard

FRUIT & NUT FILLING:
¾ cup (180 ml) kasha
⅓ cup (80 ml) chopped walnuts
⅓ cup (80 ml) diced dates
⅓ cup (80 ml) diced raisins
⅓ cup (80 ml) honey
1 tsp (5 ml) cinnamon
¼ tsp (1 ml) nutmeg

Pastry: Combine the flour and salt in a medium bowl. Make a well in the center. Add 1 egg, oil and half of the water. Stir with a wooden spoon, adding the remainder of the water to make a smooth, pliable dough. Turn the dough out onto a lightly floured board; knead a few times. Brush the dough with oil; cover with plastic wrap and let rest for about 1 hour.

At this point the dough may be refrigerated overnight. Roll the dough on a floured board, to an 18-inch square or as thin as possible. Brush the dough with oil. Cut into 36 3-inch squares or rounds. Brush the center of each with oil and fill with approximately 1 full tsp of filling; moisten the edges with water; fold over; seal the edges.

Place on a lightly greased baking sheet. Brush the tops with the beaten egg white. Bake at 375°F (190°C) for 12-15 minutes or until lightly browned. Yields 36 snack-size knishes.

Onion Filling: Sauté the onion in the butter or margarine; add the kasha and seasoning. Use to fill knishes. Bake as above. Yields 1¼ cups.

Chicken Filling: Combine all ingredients and use to fill knishes. Bake as above. Yields 1¾ cups.

Egg Filling: Combine all ingredients and use to fill knishes. Bake as above. Yields 1½ cups.

Fruit & Nut Filling: Combine all ingredients and use to fill knishes. Bake as above. Yields 1½ cups.

Approximate nutritional analysis per onion knish:
Calories 46, Protein 1 g, Carbohydrates 7 g, Fat 2 g, Cholesterol 7 mg, Sodium 38 mg

Approximate nutritional analysis per chicken knish:
Calories 51, Protein 2 g, Carbohydrates 6 g, Fat 2 g, Cholesterol 8 mg, Sodium 41 mg

Approximate nutritional analysis per egg knish:
Calories 46, Protein 2 g, Carbohydrates 7 g, Fat 1 g, Cholesterol 21 mg, Sodium 49 mg

Approximate nutritional analysis per fruit & nut knish:
Calories 64, Protein 1 g, Carbohydrates 11 g, Fat 2 g, Cholesterol 5 mg, Sodium 32 mg

KASHA-ALMOND KUGEL

2 tbsp (30 ml) butter or margarine
½ cup (120 ml) finely chopped onion
1 cup (240 ml) kasha, fine granulation
5 eggs
2 cups (480 ml) water
1 tsp (5 ml) salt
½ cup (120 ml) sugar
½ cup (120 ml) flour
1 tsp (5 ml) ground cinnamon
pinch ground nutmeg
15 pitted prunes, cooked, drained and cut into quarters
1 apple, peeled, cored and shredded
½ cup (120 ml) slivered almonds, finely chopped

Melt butter in medium skillet. Add onion and cook until tender, about 5 minutes. Toss kasha with 1 beaten egg and add to onion in pan. Stir and separate kasha as it cooks. Stir in water and salt and bring to boil; cover and cook over low heat for 10 minutes. Cool.

Meanwhile separate remaining 4 eggs. Beat whites until stiff; set aside. In large mixing bowl beat yolks until thick. Gradually add sugar, beating after each addition. Add kasha mixture. In medium bowl combine flour, cinnamon, nutmeg, prunes and apple. Stir into batter. Add nuts. Fold in beaten egg whites. Spoon into well-greased and floured 9-inch Bundt pan or ring mold. Bake at 350°F (180°C) for 40-45 minutes. Cool 15 minutes before removing from pan. Serve warm. Serves 10.

Approximate nutritional analysis per serving:
Calories 262, Protein 8 g, Carbohydrates 41 g, Fat 9 g, Cholesterol 100 mg, Sodium 270 mg

GOLDEN TOMATO-VEGETABLE RISOTTO

3½ cups (840 ml) low-sodium chicken broth
3-oz pkg (90 g) dried yellow tomatoes
2 tbsp (30 ml) olive oil
2 cups (480 ml) diced vegetables, such as zucchini, carrots,
*   red or green bell peppers, asparagus or mushrooms*
1 clove elephant garlic, minced
6-oz pkg (180 g) risotto mix
1 tbsp (15 ml) chopped fresh herbs, such as basil, chervil, chives, sage,
*   marjoram or oregano*
⅓ cup (80 ml) grated Parmesan or Romano cheese

In medium saucepan bring broth to boil; add tomatoes. Reduce heat and simmer 2 minutes. Drain tomatoes out, reserving liquid in saucepan; keep broth warm. Sliver tomatoes; set aside.

   In large saucepan or deep skillet heat olive oil. Sauté vegetables and garlic for 3-5 minutes or until vegetables are tender. Stir in risotto and tomatoes, coating well with olive oil. Add 1 cup of hot broth; cook over medium heat, stirring constantly, until broth is nearly absorbed. Repeat, adding broth and cooking liquid until rice is tender and nearly all liquid has cooked away, about 18-25 minutes. Remove from heat; stir in herbs and Parmesan cheese and season to taste with pepper. Serves 4.

Approximate nutritional analysis per serving:
Calories 209, Protein 8 g, Carbohydrates 33 g, Fat 7 g, Cholesterol 4 mg, Sodium 437 mg

NORTH BEACH RISOTTO SAFFRON

5 cups (1.2 l) vegetable broth
½ tsp (3 ml) powdered saffron
½ cup (120 ml) minced shallots
¼ lb (115 g) unsalted butter
1 garlic clove, minced
1½ cups (355 ml) Arborio rice, uncooked
½ cup (120 ml) dry white wine
1 cup (240 ml) artichoke hearts, cooked and julienned,
    or fresh asparagus, cooked firm and cut into 1-inch lengths,
    or broccoli florets, cooked firm
1 cup (240 ml) shredded Parmesan cheese

In a saucepan bring the vegetable broth to a boil over high heat. Lower the heat and keep the broth at a low simmer during the rest of the cooking time. Remove ½ cup of the broth, stir the saffron into it and set aside.

In a separate 2½-quart saucepan sauté the minced shallots until translucent in 7 tbsp butter. Add the garlic and rice. Sauté until opaque and pearl-like for 1-2 minutes. Stir in the white wine and cook. Stir constantly for about 3 minutes until the wine has evaporated.

Add ½ cup of the simmering broth to the rice, stirring constantly with a wooden spoon and waiting until the broth is absorbed before adding more. Continue adding broth ½ cup at a time until rice is cooked but still al dente, about 20-25 minutes. Use the saffron-flavored broth after the first 15 minutes of cooking. All broth may not be needed. Never let the rice stick to the bottom of the pan.

Stir in the artichoke hearts, cheese and 1 tbsp butter 1-2 minutes before the rice is done. Add salt and pepper to taste. Serves 6.

Approximate nutritional analysis per ½-cup serving:
Calories 242, Protein 8 g, Carbohydrates 31 g, Fat 8 g, Cholesterol 23 mg, Sodium 473 mg

RISOTTO & VEGETABLES

2 tbsp (30 ml) butter
1 tbsp (15 ml) olive oil
½ cup (120 ml) chopped onion
⅓ cup (80 ml) finely diced celery
⅓ cup (80 ml) finely diced carrot
½ tsp (3 ml) salt
1½ cups (355 ml) Arborio rice, uncooked
2 cups (480 ml) hot chicken broth (140°F [60°C])
2 cups (480 ml) hot water (140°F [60°C])
1 medium zucchini, finely diced
¾ cup (180 ml) frozen peas, thawed
⅓ cup (80 ml) Parmesan cheese

Combine 1 tbsp butter and olive oil in large, heavy saucepan. Add onion and cook until golden. Add celery and carrots; cook for 2-3 minutes. Add salt and rice, stirring to coat. Add 3 cups of liquid, 1 cup at a time, using all of the broth and then water; cook and stir until all liquid is absorbed before adding next cup. Add diced zucchini. Add peas with remaining water, stirring it in ½ cup at a time (all may not be needed), until last liquid is absorbed. Rice should be tender, yet firm, with creamy sauce. Remove from heat; stir in remaining 1 tbsp butter and Parmesan cheese. Serves 6.

Approximate nutritional analysis per serving:
Calories 178, Protein 6 g, Carbohydrates 28 g, Fat 6 g, Cholesterol 10 mg, Sodium 405 mg

ANTIPASTO RICE

1¾ cups (415 ml) water
½ cup (120 ml) tomato juice
1 cup (240 ml) wild rice, uncooked
1 tsp (5 ml) dried basil
1 tsp (5 ml) dried oregano
½ tsp (3 ml) salt
14-oz can (420 g) artichoke hearts, drained and quartered
7-oz jar (210 g) roasted red peppers, drained and chopped
2¼-oz can (68 g) sliced ripe black olives, drained
2 tbs (30 ml) snipped parsley
2 tbs (30 ml) lemon juice
½ tsp (3 ml) ground black pepper
2 tbsp (30 ml) grated Parmesan cheese

Combine water, tomato juice, rice, basil, oregano and salt in a 3-quart saucepan. Bring to a boil. Stir. Reduce heat; cover and simmer 45 minutes or until liquid is absorbed. Stir in artichokes, red peppers, olives, parsley, lemon juice and black pepper. Cook 5 minutes longer. Sprinkle with cheese. Serves 8.

Approximate nutritional analysis per serving:
Calories 131, Protein 4 g, Carbohydrates 27 g, Fat 2 g, Cholesterol 1 mg, Sodium 522 mg

Beans & Legumes

CURRIED BAKED BEANS

1 lb (455 g) small dry white beans
6 cups (1.4 l) water
1 tsp (5 ml) salt
2 medium apples, cored and pared
½ cup (120 ml) golden raisins
1 small onion, minced
⅓ cup (80 ml) sweet pickle relish
⅔ cup (160 ml) buckwheat honey
1 tbsp (15 ml) prepared mustard
1 tsp (5 ml) curry powder

Combine beans, water and salt in large saucepan. Let stand overnight. Bring to boil over high heat. Reduce to low and simmer 2 hours, adding water if needed. Drain beans, reserving liquid.

Combine beans with remaining ingredients. Pour into 2½-quart casserole. Add enough bean liquid to barely cover. Bake, covered, at 300°F (150°C) for 1 hour. Remove cover; bake about 30 minutes, adding more liquid if needed. Serves 10.

Approximate nutritional analysis per serving:
Calories 278, Protein 10 g, Carbohydrates 61 g, Fat .8 g, Cholesterol 0 mg, Sodium 298 mg

SOYBEAN-LENTIL-RICE LOAF

1 cup (240 ml) cooked soybeans
1 cup (240 ml) cooked lentils
1 cup (240 ml) cooked brown rice
¾ cup (180 ml) soy milk, water, stock or gravy
1 medium onion, finely chopped
2 cloves garlic, finely chopped
2 egg whites, beaten
¼ cup (60 ml) tomato purée plus additional, for serving
2 stalks celery, chopped
1 cup (240 ml) wheat germ
½ tsp (3 ml) onion powder
½ tsp (3 ml) chile powder
2 tsp (10 ml) sea salt, optional

In a large mixing bowl mash the soybeans and lentils well. Add the rest of the ingredients and mix well. Turn into an oiled loaf pan. Bake in a preheated 325°F (165°C) oven for 1 hour. Serve as is or top with the additional tomato purée. Serves 4.

Approximate nutritional analysis per serving:
Calories 287, Protein 20 g, Carbohydrates 41 g, Fat 6 g, Cholesterol 0 mg, Sodium 104 mg

NAVY BEAN TARRAGON

1 tbsp (15 ml) olive oil
1 cup (240 ml) finely diced onion
1 cup (240 ml) quartered mushrooms
1 cup (240 ml) thinly sliced scallions
1 cup (240 ml) thinly sliced leeks
¾ tsp (4 ml) dried tarragon leaves
1½ cups (355 ml) cooked navy beans
½ cup (120 ml) white wine
¼ cup (60 ml) soy beverage powder
4½ tsp (23 ml) dark miso
1 tbsp (15 ml) fresh lemon juice
3 tbsp (45 ml) diced red bell pepper, optional
3 tbsp (45 ml) sliced scallions, optional

Heat a sauté pan on medium heat for 1 minute and add the oil, onion, mushrooms, scallions, leeks and tarragon; sauté until the onions are transparent. Add the beans. Blend the wine, soy beverage powder, miso and lemon juice together until smooth. Add this mixture to the sautéed vegetables and simmer gently for 5 minutes. Serve as is or over cooked pasta or grain. Garnish with the bell pepper and/or scallions. Serves 5.

Approximate nutritional analysis per serving:
Calories 209, Protein 9 g, Carbohydrates 31 g, Fat 5 g, Cholesterol 0 mg, Sodium 241 mg

BLACK BEANS & COUSCOUS

1 cup (240 ml) black beans, soaked overnight
1-2 bay leaves
6-8 cloves garlic, minced
2 tsp (10 ml) dried oregano
1 tsp (5 ml) cumin
red pepper, optional
1 tbsp (15 ml) baking soda
1 tsp (5 ml) salt
1 cup (240 ml) raw couscous

In saucepan place beans and bay leaves in enough water to cover beans and bring to boil. Reduce heat and simmer for 1½ hours or until beans are tender. Add garlic, oregano, cumin, red pepper and black pepper to taste. Add additional water so that beans remain covered. Simmer 30 minutes more or until beans are softened, add baking soda and salt and mix well. Correct seasoning to taste. Continue to cook until soup thickens to desired consistency. Adjust with additional water if necessary. Meanwhile steam couscous. Serve couscous with ladle of black beans. Serves 6.

Approximate nutritional analysis per serving:
Calories 226, Protein 9 g, Carbohydrates 46 g, Fat .4 g, Cholesterol 0 mg, Sodium 638 mg

STIR-FRIED LENTILS & BEANS

¼ cup (60 ml) sesame oil
½ cup (120 ml) diced onion
½ cup (120 ml) diced celery
1 cup (240 ml) sliced mushrooms
2 cups (480 ml) cooked red lentils
1 cup (240 ml) cooked adzuki beans
½ cup (120 ml) fresh mung bean sprouts
½ cup (120 ml) sliced water chestnuts
2 tsp (10 ml) low-sodium tamari sauce
½ tsp (3 ml) marjoram
¼ tsp (1 ml) nutmeg
¼ tsp (1 ml) garlic powder
¼ tsp (1 ml) onion powder

Heat the oil in a large skillet or wok and sauté the onion, celery and mushrooms until brown. Add the remaining ingredients and cook, stirring until heated through. Serves 6.

Approximate nutritional analysis per serving:
Calories 225, Protein 10 g, Carbohydrates 27 g, Fat 9 g, Cholesterol 0 mg, Sodium 105 mg

QUICK BEAN STIR-FRY WITH RICE

½ cup (120 ml) chopped scallions or onion
⅓ cup (80 ml) chopped celery
½ cup (120 ml) chopped green pepper
2 cloves minced garlic
3 tbsp (45 ml) cooking oil
2-3 cups (480-720 ml) cooked yellow-eye beans
½ cup(120 ml) tomato purée
½ tsp (3 ml) dry basil
¼ cup (60 ml) grated carrots, for garnish
2 cups (480 ml) cooked brown rice, optional

Sauté scallions, celery, green pepper and garlic in oil for 1-2 minutes to soften. Add beans and stir-fry for 1-2 minutes more, then add tomato purée, basil and salt and pepper to taste. Continue to cook over medium heat, stirring frequently, for about 10 minutes. Correct seasoning. Place in serving dish and garnish with grated carrots. Can be served next to or over rice. Serves 4.

Approximate nutritional analysis per serving:
Calories 339, Protein 11 g, Carbohydrates 48 g, Fat 12 g, Cholesterol 2 mg, Sodium 19 mg

MARROW BEANS WITH RICE

8-oz pkg (240 g) dried marrow beans
1 tbsp (15 ml) vegetable oil
1 cup (240 ml) chopped onion
2 cloves garlic, minced
1 fresh Anaheim chile, seeded and minced
3 cups (720 ml) chicken broth or water
2 tomatoes, chopped
1 cup (240 ml) wild, brown or white rice
1 bay leaf
1 tbsp (15 ml) chopped basil
1 tsp (5 ml) grated orange peel
½ tsp (3 ml) salt
¼ tsp (1 ml) pepper

In a large saucepan cover beans with water. Bring to a boil; boil 2 minutes. Remove from heat; cover and let stand 1 hour. Drain beans; in same pan heat oil. Sauté onion, garlic and chile in oil for 5 minutes or until vegetables are tender. Stir in drained beans, broth, tomatoes, rice, bay leaf, basil and orange peel. Bring mixture to a boil. Reduce heat, cover and simmer for 45-50 minutes or until beans and rice are tender and all liquid is absorbed. Remove bay leaf; stir in salt and pepper. Serves 6 as a main dish.

Approximate nutritional analysis per serving:
Calories 250, Protein 13 g, Carbohydrates 45 g, Fat 3 g, Cholesterol 0 mg, Sodium 189 mg

YELLOW-EYE BEANS & SQUASH STEW

8-oz pkg dried yellow-eye beans
1 tbsp (15 ml) olive oil
1 cup (240 ml) chopped onion
1 red or green bell pepper
2 cloves garlic, minced
14½-oz can (435 ml) chicken broth
2 cups (480 ml) water
2 cups (480 ml) diced tomatoes
1 lb (455 g) acorn, butternut, banana or pumpkin squash,
*   peeled, seeded and cut into 1-inch chunks*
1 tbsp (15 ml) chopped fresh oregano
2 tsp (10 ml) chopped fresh thyme
½ tsp (3 ml) salt
¼ tsp (1 ml) pepper

Place beans in a 2-quart saucepan. Cover with 2 inches of water and bring to a boil. Cook for 2 minutes; remove from heat. Cover; let stand for 1 hour. Drain beans. In a large Dutch oven heat oil; sauté onion, bell pepper and garlic for 5-10 minutes or until vegetables are tender. Stir in drained beans, broth, water, tomatoes, squash, oregano and thyme. Bring to a boil; reduce heat. Simmer, partially covered, for 1-1½ hours or until beans are tender. Stir in salt and pepper. Serves 6 as a main dish.

Approximate nutritional analysis per serving:
Calories 132, Protein 7 g, Carbohydrates 20 g, Fat 3 g, Cholesterol 0 mg, Sodium 405 mg

APPALOOSA BEANS & CORN

8-oz pkg (240 g) dried appaloosa beans
1 tbsp (15 ml) vegetable oil
1 cup (240 ml) chopped onion
2 cloves garlic, minced
2 cups (480 ml) chicken broth or water
1½ cups (355 ml) niblet corn
2 tsp (10 ml) chopped fresh sage
½ tsp (3 ml) salt
¼ tsp (1 ml) pepper

Place beans in 2-quart saucepan. Cover with 2 inches of water and bring to boil. Cook for 2 minutes; reduce heat. Simmer, partially covered, about 2 hours or until beans are just tender, making sure water does not cook out. Drain beans. Remove beans from pan and set them aside.

In same saucepan heat oil; sauté onion and garlic for 5 minutes or until vegetables are tender. Stir in drained beans, broth, corn and sage. Cook 10-15 minutes or until mixture is heated through. Stir in salt and pepper. Serves 4 as main dish.

Approximate nutritional analysis per serving:
Calories 175, Protein 7 g, Carbohydrates 30 g, Fat 4 g, Cholesterol 0 mg, Sodium 145 mg

CURRIED GARBANZO BEANS & RICE

2 tbsp (30 ml) olive oil
1 medium onion, chopped
1 medium green bell pepper, diced
2 15-oz cans (900 g) garbanzo beans, drained and rinsed
2-4 cloves garlic, finely chopped
2 tsp (10 ml) curry powder
½ cup (120 ml) water
14-oz can (420 g) plum tomatoes, chopped, liquid reserved
2 10-oz pkgs (600 g) frozen chopped spinach, thawed and squeezed dry

In large saucepan heat oil. Add onion and green pepper; cook over medium heat, stirring occasionally, 3-5 minutes. Add beans, garlic, curry powder and water; bring to simmer, cover and cook 5 minutes. Stir in tomatoes and their liquid. Add spinach and cover and cook 10 minutes. Salt to taste. Serve over cooked rice. Serves 6.

Approximate nutritional analysis per serving:
Calories 265, Protein 11 g, Carbohydrates 44 g, Fat 7 g, Cholesterol 0 mg, Sodium 512 mg

LENTIL CURRY

1½ cups (355 ml) lentils, washed and drained
6 cups (1.4 l) water
1 tbsp (15 ml) vegetable oil
1 cup (240 ml) chopped onion
2 cloves garlic, minced
1 tsp (15 ml) curry powder
1 tsp (5 ml) cumin seeds
2 14½-oz cans (870 g) diced tomatoes, undrained
1 green apple, diced
½ cup (120 ml) seedless raisins
3 cups (720 ml) cooked couscous or rice
2 tbsp (30 ml) chopped fresh cilantro or parsley, for garnish

In large saucepan combine lentils and water. Bring to boil; reduce heat to low and simmer, partially covered, 45-50 minutes or until lentils are tender, occasionally skimming off foam and stirring to prevent sticking.

In large skillet heat oil over medium heat. Add onion, garlic, curry powder and cumin seeds; cook until onion is tender. Stir in tomatoes, apple and raisins. Season with salt and pepper. When lentils are tender, stir into onion mixture; cook, covered, about 15 minutes or until apple is tender. Serve over hot cooked couscous, garnished with cilantro. Serves 6.

Approximate nutritional analysis per serving:
Calories 379, Protein 19 g, Carbohydrates 70 g, Fat 3 g, Cholesterol 0 mg, Sodium 217 mg

LENTIL LOAF

2 cups (480 ml) cooked red or green lentils
1 cup (240 ml) cooked brown rice
1 cup (240 ml) cooked bulgur wheat
1 cup (240 ml) garbanzo flour
⅔ cup (180 ml) cold water
½-1 cup (120-240 ml) chopped nuts
1 tbsp (15 ml) soy sauce
1 tsp (5 ml) sage
1 tbsp (15 ml) unrefined vegetable oil
1 tsp (5 ml) sea salt, optional

Drain the cooked lentils and grains. Mix the flour and water, then all ingredients together. Spoon into a loaf pan. Bake at 350°F (180°C) for 30-45 minutes. Serve with any leftover gravy over top. Serves 6.

Approximate nutritional analysis per serving:
Calories 306, Protein 15 g, Carbohydrates 42 g, Fat 10 g, Cholesterol 0 mg, Sodium 184 mg

TOASTED GARBANZO PATTIES

1½ cups (355 ml) garbanzo flour
1 cup (240 ml) water
1 medium onion, finely chopped
½ cup (120 ml) oat flakes
½ cup (120 ml) ground pecans or other nuts
1 tbsp (15 ml) parsley
1 tsp (5 ml) savory
1 tsp (5 ml) salt
toasted sesame oil or other oil

Mix flour and water. Let sit while preparing remaining ingredients. Combine all other ingredients together, mixing well. When mixture is quite thick, shape into patties. Fry lightly on both sides in oil. Flatten patties fairly thin while cooking. Serves 6.

Approximate nutritional analysis per serving:
Calories 207, Protein 8 g, Carbohydrates 28 g, Fat 9 g, Cholesterol 0 mg, Sodium 49 mg

Pasta & Noodles

ORIENTAL RIGATONI WITH CHICKEN

8 oz (240 g) rigatoni
1 lb (455 g) skinless, boneless chicken breasts
1 tsp (5 ml) vegetable oil
pinch cayenne pepper
1 bunch green onion, cut into 1-inch diagonals
1½ cups (355 ml) pineapple juice
1 tbsp (15 ml) chopped fresh gingerroot
1 tbsp (15 ml) honey
1 tbsp (15 ml) butter or margarine
1 tbsp (15 ml) lemon juice
1 tbsp (15 ml) chopped fresh cilantro or 1 tsp (5 ml) dried cilantro
1 tbsp (15 ml) pine nuts, toasted

Prepare the pasta according to package directions and drain. Brush the chicken with the vegetable oil and season with the cayenne pepper. Bake at 350°F (180°C) until cooked through, about 30 minutes. During the last 10 minutes place the green onion in the pan. Combine the pineapple juice, ginger and honey in a small saucepan. Bring to a boil over medium-high heat and reduce by half. Whisk in the butter or margarine and the lemon juice. Toss the pasta with the chicken and scallions and add the sauce. Garnish with the cilantro and pine nuts and serve immediately. Serves 4.

Approximate nutritional analysis per serving:
Calories 477, Protein 35 g, Carbohydrates 64 g, Fat 8 g, Cholesterol 74 mg, Sodium 110 mg

BROCCOLI & RED PEPPER TORTELLINI

1 lb (455 g) cheese tortellini
3 tbsp (45 ml) olive oil
1 lb (455 g) broccoli florets
2 large sweet red peppers, julienned
3-4 cloves garlic, crushed
2-3 tbsp (30-45 ml) red wine vinegar

Cook tortellini according to package directions and drain. Heat the olive oil in a heavy skillet. Sauté the broccoli and peppers until they are slightly tender, about 3-4 minutes. Add the garlic and cook 1 minute more. Add the vinegar, raise the heat and cook 1 minute more. Stir in the tortellini and heat thoroughly, about 1 minute. Serves 4.

Approximate nutritional analysis per serving:
Calories 375, Protein 17 g, Carbohydrates 37 g, Fat 19 g, Cholesterol 147 mg, Sodium 288 mg

PENNE PEPPER PASTA

3 cups (720 ml) penne pasta, uncooked
3 peppers (1 red, 1 yellow and 1 green), cut into strips
2 scallions, trimmed and finely chopped
¼ cup (60 ml) finely chopped fresh basil
1 tbsp (15 ml) paprika
1 tbsp (15 ml) garlic-flavored oil
3 tbsp (45 ml) balsamic vinegar
½ cup (120 ml) kalamata olives
1½ tbsp (25 ml) extra-virgin olive oil
grated mozzarella cheese

In large pot of boiling water cook penne until al dente, about 6-8 minutes. Drain in colander and rinse well with cold water. Transfer to large bowl and set aside.

Sauté peppers, scallions, basil and paprika in garlic oil in pan until peppers are soft and glistening. Remove from heat and add balsamic vinegar. Spoon pepper mixture over pasta and toss with olives and olive oil. Season with black pepper and grated mozzarella. Serves 6.

Approximate nutritional analysis per serving:
Calories 281, Protein 7 g, Carbohydrates 43 g, Fat 9 g, Cholesterol 0 mg, Sodium 456 mg

PASTA E PISELLI

½ cup (120 ml) chopped onion
4 slices bacon
2 tbsp (30 ml) butter
1 cup (240 ml) low-sodium chicken broth
1 lb (455 g) shelled peas
1 lb (455 g) fettucini
1 cup (240 ml) grated Parmesan cheese

Sauté onion and bacon in butter. Remove bacon and place on paper towel to drain. Add chicken broth to pan along with peas and cover. Cook over very low flame with lid on pan until onion is limp and liquid is almost gone.

Cook fettucini and drain while onion is cooking. Both should be finished at same time, about 20 minutes. Crumble bacon and combine bacon, onion and peas with fettucini. Sprinkle with Parmesan cheese and toss. Serves 8.

Approximate nutritional analysis per serving:
Calories 235, Protein 13 g, Carbohydrates 26 g, Fat 9 g, Cholesterol 20 mg, Sodium 390 mg

SMOKY CHIPOTLE PASTA

1 tbsp (15 ml) olive or vegetable oil
1 cup (240 ml) slivered zucchini or yellow squash
1 cup (240 ml) slivered red or green bell pepper
1½ cups (355 ml) low-sodium chicken or beef broth
⅓ cup (80 ml) chopped onion
1 clove garlic, minced
3-oz pkg (90 g) dried tomatoes, rehydrated and chopped
¼ cup (60 ml) chipotle chile, rehydrated and minced
¼ cup (60 ml) chopped fresh cilantro,
 plus additional sprigs for garnish
1 tbsp (15 ml) chopped fresh oregano
 or 1 tsp (5 ml) crushed dried oregano
¼ tsp (1 ml) pepper
½ cup (120 ml) low-sodium niblet corn
1¾ cups (415 ml) julienned cooked or grilled chicken breast
½ lb (230 g) pasta of choice, cooked and drained

In large skillet heat oil. Sauté zucchini and bell pepper 3 minutes, turning often. In blender container or food processor bowl place half of broth, onion, garlic, half of tomatoes, chile, cilantro, oregano and pepper. Cover and process until smooth. Add mixture to skillet with remaining broth and tomato pieces, corn and chicken pieces. Simmer over low heat until heated through. Toss with drained cooked pasta; garnish with fresh cilantro sprigs. Serves 4.

Approximate nutritional analysis per serving:
Calories 305, Protein 26 g, Carbohydrates 37 g, Fat 7 g, Cholesterol 52 mg, Sodium 495 mg

SUNNY TORTELLINI

1 lb (455 g) cheese-filled spinach tortellini
2 cups (480 ml) nonfat plain yogurt
¼ cup (60 ml) finely chopped sun-dried tomatoes
2 scallions, chopped
½ tsp (3 ml) dried thyme
dash tamari or soy sauce
freshly ground black pepper
1 large onion, chopped
2 shallots, chopped
2 cloves garlic, crushed
3-5 tbsp (45-75 ml) vegetable oil
1½ lbs (683 g) mushrooms, sliced

Boil water for the tortellini. Combine the yogurt, tomatoes, scallions, thyme, tamari and pepper to taste. Mix well and set aside. Cook the tortellini according to package directions.

While the tortellini are cooking, sauté the onion, shallots and garlic in oil. Add the mushrooms and continue cooking, stirring occasionally, for 15-20 minutes or until wilted.

When the tortellini are done, drain them and return them to a pot. Add the mushroom mixture immediately and toss. Add the yogurt mixture, stirring to coat the pasta and mushrooms. Serve immediately. Serves 4.

Approximate nutritional analysis per serving:
Calories 447, Protein 23 g, Carbohydrates 48 g, Fat 20 g, Cholesterol 149 mg, Sodium 413 mg

VEGETABLE PASTA PRIMAVERA

1 lb (455 g) pasta, uncooked

WHITE SAUCE:
4 cups (960 ml) water
4 vegetable bouillon cubes
1½ cups (355 ml) instant soy beverage
4 rounded tbsp (60 ml) cornstarch

¼ cup (60 ml) canola oil
1½ cups (355 ml) broccoli florets
1½ cups (355 ml) sliced carrots
1 cup (240 ml) diced celery
1½ cups (355 ml) onion wedges
1½ cups (355 ml) cauliflower florets
1 cup (240 ml) peas

Cook pasta according to package directions and drain.

Meanwhile blend white sauce ingredients and cook in saucepan on medium heat. Stir until thickened.

In large skillet sauté vegetables in canola oil until al dente.

Pour white sauce over vegetable mix. Place pasta on plate and pour vegetables and sauce on top. Serves 8.

Approximate nutritional analysis per serving:
Calories 309, Protein 11 g, Carbohydrates 41 g, Fat 12 g, Cholesterol .1 mg, Sodium 421 mg

VEGETABLE PASTA-YOGURT TOSS

2 tbsp (45 ml) olive oil
3 cloves garlic, minced
3-4 carrots, peeled and diagonally cut
1 medium onion, sliced
¼ head red cabbage, shredded
1 red bell pepper, cored, seeded and chopped
1 tsp (5 ml) caraway seeds
¼ cup (60 ml) water
1 tsp (5 ml) cider vinegar
1 lb spinach pasta, any kind
¾ cup (180 ml) sliced mushrooms
1 tsp (5 ml) dried dill
¼ tsp (1 ml) white pepper

SAUCE:
1 tbsp (15 ml) olive oil
1 tbsp (15 ml) butter
1 cup (240 ml) nonfat plain yogurt
1 tbsp (15 ml) cornstarch
1 cup (240 ml) grated sharp cheddar cheese

Heat the olive oil over medium-high heat in a large skillet. Add the garlic and cook until softened. Add the carrots and sauté for 2-3 minutes. Add the onion, red cabbage, bell pepper and caraway seeds. Sauté for 1 minute. Add the water and vinegar; stir to combine. Continue cooking; when water boils and begins to steam, cover the pan and reduce the heat to medium-low. Cook for 10 minutes.

Meanwhile cook pasta according to package directions.

Add the mushrooms, dill and white pepper to the cabbage mixture. Cover and cook for 5 more minutes.

To make the sauce combine the olive oil, butter, yogurt and cornstarch in a small saucepan. Stir constantly over medium-low heat. Add the cheese gradually while continuing to stir. Simmer gently for 1 minute.

When the pasta is done, drain it and return it to the cooking pot. Add the vegetables and toss. Add the yogurt sauce and toss again. Serve immediately. Serves 4.

Approximate nutritional analysis per serving:
Calories 744, Protein 28 g, Carbohydrates 103 g, Fat 25 g, Cholesterol 39 mg, Sodium 312 mg

PASTA E FAGIOLI WITH BASIL

olive oil spray
1 medium onion, chopped
4 cloves garlic, chopped
½ lb (230 g) mushrooms, sliced
1 red bell pepper, chopped
2 stalks celery, sliced
2 14½-oz cans (870 g) low-sodium ready-cut tomatoes, with juice
2 15-oz cans (900 g) cannellini, red kidney or great northern beans,
  rinsed and drained
½ lb (230 g) spinach leaves, coarsely chopped
1 small bunch fresh basil, chopped, some reserved for garnish
1 lb (455 g) ziti, cooked al dente
grated Parmesan cheese, optional

Coat nonstick skillet with olive oil cooking spray. Sauté onion, garlic, mushrooms, bell pepper and celery for 5 minutes or until soft. Reduce heat and add tomatoes with juice and beans. Add water to reach desired consistency. Cover and simmer for 15 minutes. Add spinach, basil and salt and pepper to taste. Simmer 15 more minutes. Toss with additional chopped basil for garnish and serve over hot pasta with Parmesan cheese. Serves 8.

Approximate nutritional analysis per serving:
Calories 384, Protein 19 g, Carbohydrates 75 g, Fat 2 g, Cholesterol .5 mg, Sodium 199 mg

LINGUINE WITH HONEY-SAUCED PRAWNS

8 oz (240 g) prawns, peeled and deveined
¼ cup (60 ml) julienned carrots
¼ cup (60 ml) julienned celery
¼ cup (60 ml) diagonally sliced green onion
3 cloves garlic, minced
1 tbsp (15 ml) olive oil
¼ cup (60 ml) water
2 tbsp (15 ml) honey
2 tsp (10 ml) cornstarch
½ tsp (3 ml) salt
pinch crushed dried red chile
pinch rosemary
2½ cups (590 ml) warm cooked linguine

In medium skillet stir-fry prawns, carrots, celery, green onion and garlic in oil about 3 minutes or until shrimp start to turn pink. Combine remaining ingredients, except linguine, in small bowl and mix well. Add to vegetable mixture; stir-fry about 1 minute or until sauce thickens. Serve over linguine. Serves 2.

Approximate nutritional analysis per serving:
Calories 512, Protein 33 g, Carbohydrates 74 g, Fat 9 g, Cholesterol 221 mg, Sodium 810 mg

SHRIMP WITH HONEY CREAM SAUCE & SPINACH PASTA

2 tbsp (30 ml) olive oil
1 lb (455 g) medium shrimp, peeled and deveined
2 tbsp (30 ml) chopped shallots
½ cup (120 ml) dry white wine
½ cup (120 ml) heavy cream
2 tbsp (30 ml) honey
½ cup (120 ml) peeled, seeded and diced fresh plum tomatoes
*   or drained, diced canned plum tomatoes*
2 tbsp (30 ml) chopped fresh basil
½ lb (230 g) spinach fettucini, cooked and drained
basil sprigs, for garnish, optional

Heat olive oil in large skillet over medium-high heat. Add shrimp and shallots, tossing lightly, until shrimp are just opaque. Remove shrimp and keep warm. Add wine to pan; boil until liquid is reduced by half, stirring and scraping sides of pan. Add cream and reduce heat to medium; cook until slightly thickened. Add honey, tomatoes and chopped basil; stir to blend. Return shrimp to sauce and season with salt and pepper to taste. Arrange equal portions of fettucini and shrimp mixture on warm serving plates. Garnish with basil sprigs. Serves 4.

Approximate nutritional analysis per serving:
Calories 547, Protein 32 g, Carbohydrates 54 g, Fat 20 g, Cholesterol 262 mg, Sodium 290 mg

STIR-FRIED NOODLES WITH SHRIMP

12-oz pkg (360 g) Chinese-style noodles
½ lb (230 g) Chinese cabbage
4 tbsp (60 ml) vegetable oil
1 lb (455 g) uncooked shrimp, shelled, deveined and
sliced in half lengthwise
1 tsp salt
1 tbsp (15 ml) Chinese rice wine or sherry
1 tsp (5 ml) honey or other sweetener
1 tbsp (15 ml) low-sodium soy sauce
½ cup (120 ml) low-sodium vegetable or chicken stock

Cook noodles as package directs. Wash cabbage and slice each stalk lengthwise into ⅛-inch-wide strips. Heat wok or skillet. Pour in half the oil. On medium heat stir-fry shrimp 1 minute or until they turn pink. Add ½ tsp salt and rice wine, stir, then transfer to plate and set aside. Pour rest of oil into hot pan and stir-fry cabbage for 2 minutes. Add ½ tsp salt, honey, noodles, soy sauce and stock and boil briskly for 3 minutes or until liquid has evaporated. Add shrimp and cook, stirring, for 30 seconds. Serve at once. Serves 5.

Approximate nutritional analysis per serving:
Calories 408, Protein 27 g, Carbohydrates 45 g, Fat 12 g, Cholesterol 177 mg, Sodium 639 mg

STIR-FRIED NOODLES & SHRIMP

1¼ cups (295 ml) small shell pasta, uncooked
¼ lb (115 g) fresh snow peas
½ lb (230 g) cooked medium shrimp
2-3 tbsp (30-45 ml) olive oil
1 clove garlic, minced
1-2 tbsp (15-30 ml) minced fresh dill
⅓ cup (80 ml) freshly grated Parmesan cheese

Cook pasta shells, rinse with cool water and drain. Steam peas until crisp-tender. Combine shrimp, olive oil, garlic and dill in small skillet and cook until hot. Add pasta, peas and Parmesan cheese and toss to coat. Serves 2.

Approximate nutritional analysis per serving:
Calories 423, Protein 35 g, Carbohydrates 24 g, Fat 20 g, Cholesterol 234 mg, Sodium 568 mg

PASTA & SALMON HOT DISH

8 oz (240 g) fettucini
1 tbsp (15 ml) olive or canola oil
½ cup (120 ml) asparagus tips and pieces, cut diagonally in
*   ½-inch lengths, or thinly sliced zucchini*
½ cup (120 ml) green or red pepper, cut into ½-inch chunks
¼ cup (60 ml) sliced green onion
1 garlic clove, minced
6-oz can (180 g) salmon, drained
1 cup (240 ml) frozen peas, thawed
2 tbsp (30 ml) fresh parsley or 2 tsp (10 ml) dried parsley
½ tsp (3 ml) dried basil
½ cup (120 ml) low-fat plain yogurt
2-3 tbsp (30-45 ml) grated Parmesan cheese

Cook fettucini noodles al dente and drain. Meanwhile heat oil in large skillet. Add asparagus, pepper, onion and garlic and sauté until tender-crisp. Add salmon in chunks, peas, parsley and basil. Sauté until mixture is heated through and peas are soft. Drain pasta and add yogurt. Toss salmon mixture with pasta. Top with Parmesan cheese. Serves 4.

Approximate nutritional analysis per serving:
Calories 452, Protein 32 g, Carbohydrates 58 g, Fat 12 g, Cholesterol 44 mg, Sodium 582 mg

PASTA WITH CHICKEN

1 green bell pepper
1 red bell pepper
1 cup (240 ml) chopped broccoli
1 carrot
3 lbs (1.4 g) chicken breast
2 tbsp (30 ml) olive oil
1 medium onion
2 cloves garlic, minced
25-oz jar (750 ml) marinara-with-mushrooms sauce
1 lb (455 g) linguine, cooked and drained
2 tbsp (30 ml) chopped parsley, for garnish

Cut vegetables and chicken in bite-size pieces. Heat oil over medium-high heat. Add chicken and brown all over. Remove from pan. Sauté onion and garlic until onion is limp. Add chopped vegetables and cook 2 minutes, or steam vegetables separately; add marinara and cook for another 2 minutes. Serve warm over linguine. Garnish with chopped parsley. Serves 6.

Approximate nutritional analysis per serving:
Calories 498, Protein 60 g, Carbohydrates 38 g, Fat 10 g, Cholesterol 131 mg, Sodium 158 mg

EGG NOODLES WITH
YOGURT-VEGETABLE SAUCE

1 tbsp (15 ml) butter or oil for frying
1 small onion, chopped
1 clove garlic, finely chopped
½ cup (120 ml) sliced mushrooms
½ cup (120 ml) peeled, diced carrots
1 ear corn, sliced off cob, or ¾ cup (180 ml) frozen corn
1 cup (240 ml) diced cooked turkey and/or ham, optional
tamari or soy sauce
2 cups (480 ml) nonfat plain yogurt, at room temperature
12-oz pkg (360 g) egg noodles
paprika
zucchini, thinly sliced for garnish, optional

Heat the butter in an ovenproof skillet. Working with one ingredient at a time, and stirring after each addition, add the onion, garlic, mushrooms, carrots and corn. Sprinkle in a small amount of water as the vegetables cook so they don't become too dry. Add the meat and stir in. Add tamari to taste and stir again. When the vegetables are tender, remove from the heat, add the yogurt and stir to blend. Then place the pan of vegetables in a warm oven to blend the flavors while you cook the noodles.

Cook the egg noodles according to package directions. Drain, place in a serving dish and dot with butter. Cover with the yogurt-vegetable sauce and sprinkle with paprika. Garnish with zucchini. Serves 3.

Approximate nutritional analysis per serving:
Calories 607, Protein 27 g, Carbohydrates 105 g, Fat 7 g, Cholesterol 109 mg, Sodium 157 mg

BURGUNDY "SPAGHETTI"

1 lb (455 g) ground beef or turkey
1 medium onion, chopped
3 tbsp (45 ml) safflower oil
3 cups (720 ml) tomato sauce
½ cup (120 ml) sliced mushrooms
1 cup (240 ml) burgundy wine
2 cloves garlic, minced
½ tsp (3 ml) oregano
½ tsp (3 ml) basil
½ tsp (3 ml) rosemary
½ tsp (3 ml) marjoram
1 bay leaf, optional
½ tsp (3 ml) salt
¼ tsp (1 ml) black pepper
12 oz (240 g) angel hair pasta
2 cups (480 ml) shredded low-fat cheese

Sauté ground meat and onion in oil until meat is browned. Drain excess fat. Add all ingredients except pasta and cheese. Simmer on low at least 1 hour, stirring occasionally, until desired thickness is reached.

In the meantime add pasta to boiling water. Cook just until pasta separates, approximately 2-3 minutes. You may separate pasta carefully with fork as it cooks. Drain pasta well. Turn into sauce with approximately 1½ cups of cheese. Transfer to covered casserole dish. If you wish, you may cover and refrigerate at this point. Before serving heat oven to 325°F (165°C). Sprinkle remaining cheese, cover and bake for approximately 45 minutes. Uncover and continue baking for 30 minutes. Garlic bread and red wine go well with this meal. Serves 6.

Approximate nutritional analysis per serving:
Calories 410, Protein 29 g, Carbohydrates 29 g, Fat 19 g, Cholesterol 62 mg, Sodium 696 mg

SPANISH PASTA ROLL

PASTA:
1¼ cups (295 ml) whole grain flour
2 tbsp (30 ml) butter, melted
2 eggs, beaten
dash salt

FILLING:
2 cups (480 ml) ricotta cheese
4 oz (120 g) canned green chiles, chopped
¼ cup (60 ml) chopped fresh cilantro
¼ tsp (1 ml) oregano
¼ tsp (1 ml) salt
⅛-¼ tsp (.5-1 ml) red pepper
¾ cup (180 ml) corn kernels
¾ cup (180 ml) chopped tomatoes
¼ cup (60 ml) chopped green onion
¼ tsp (1 ml) garlic powder

Preheat oven to 375°F (190°C). Prepare pasta by making a well in the flour and pouring in the butter, eggs and salt. Mix thoroughly and roll into a ball. Keep dough covered while preparing the filling.

   Add all the filling ingredients together. Stir just until everything is coated and mixed. Roll out dough on a floured surface to fit into a 12x16-inch baking dish. Spread evenly with filling and roll like a jelly roll. Seal edges with water. Bake for approximately 25 minutes. Serves 4.

Approximate nutritional analysis per serving:
Calories 436, Protein 25 g, Carbohydrates 46 g, Fat 19 g, Cholesterol 147 mg, Sodium 479 mg

CANNELLONI

8 cannelloni or manicotti shells
15-oz carton (450 g) part-skim ricotta cheese
1½ cups (355 ml) grated low-fat mozzarella cheese
¼ cup (60 ml) freshly grated Parmesan cheese
1 egg, slightly beaten
2 tbsp (30 ml) chopped fresh parsley
dash nutmeg
26-oz jar (780 ml) pasta sauce or 3 cups (720 ml)
   homemade pasta sauce

Cook cannelloni shells according to package directions; rinse with cool water and drain well. Combine ricotta cheese, ½ cup mozzarella cheese, Parmesan cheese, egg, parsley and nutmeg. Spoon ricotta filling into shells. Preparation may be covered and refrigerated several hours at this point. Pour half of pasta sauce in bottom of 12x18-inch glass baking dish. Lay filled shells over sauce; cover with remaining sauce. Cover with aluminum foil; bake at 375°F (190°C) for 30 minutes or until sauce is bubbling. Sprinkle with remaining 1 cup mozzarella cheese. Bake, uncovered, another 5-10 minutes or until cheese has melted. Serves 4.

Approximate nutritional analysis per serving:
Calories 465, Protein 33 g, Carbohydrates 40 g, Fat 19 g, Cholesterol 107 mg, Sodium 938 mg

SEAFOOD D'ITALIA

1 medium onion, finely chopped
4 large mushrooms, thinly sliced
6 cloves garlic, crushed
2 tbsp (30 ml) olive oil
2 tbsp (30 ml) butter
1 tbsp (15 ml) capers
½ tsp (3 ml) oregano
2 tbsp (30 ml) chopped chives
8½-oz can (255 g) artichoke hearts, drained
8 oz (240 g) scallops
8 oz (230 g) whole raw shrimp, peeled and deveined
2 tbsp (30 ml) red wine vinegar
1 lb (455 g) fettucini

Sauté onion, mushrooms and garlic in olive oil and butter until soft. Add capers, herbs, pepper to taste, artichokes, scallops and shrimp and continue to simmer until seafood is cooked, 5-7 minutes at medium heat. Stir in vinegar and cook 1 minute more. Serve over fettucini, cooked al dente. Serves 8.

Approximate nutritional analysis per serving:
Calories 340, Protein 19 g, Carbohydrates 48 g, Fat 8 g, Cholesterol 72 mg, Sodium 160 mg

POTATO-GARBANZO GNOCCHI

2 cups (480 ml) boiling water
2 cups (480 ml) potato flakes
½ cup (120 ml) garbanzo flour
¼ cup (60 ml) rice flour
1 tsp (5 ml) garlic powder
pinch cayenne or red pepper
1 tsp (5 ml) non-alum baking powder, optional
1 tbsp (15 ml) smoked nutritional yeast, optional
1 tsp (5 ml) sea salt, optional

Combine water and potato flakes quickly. They will set up firmly and be somewhat dry. Stir in the remaining ingredients. Drop by the teaspoonful into hot oil and deep fry until golden brown. Omitting the baking powder will result in denser gnocchi. Serves 4.

Approximate nutritional analysis per serving:
Calories 240, Protein 6 g, Carbohydrates 37 g, Fat 8 g, Cholesterol 0 mg, Sodium 31 mg

CREAMY POLENTA WITH FRESH THYME

3 cups (720 ml) water
⅔ cup (160 ml) polenta (yellow cornmeal)
½ cup (120 ml) whole milk
2 tbsp (30 ml) fresh thyme
2 tbsp (30 ml) grated Parmesan cheese
2 medium zucchini
2 medium tomatoes
1 small eggplant
1 medium green pepper
olive oil

In a medium saucepan bring the water to a boil and add the polenta. Reduce the heat and simmer for 10 minutes. Add the milk and thyme and cook for an additional 5 minutes. Add the cheese and season with salt and pepper if you wish. Cut the vegetables crosswise in halves, season with pepper, brush lightly with olive oil and grill. Divide into even portions and serve over the polenta. Serves 3.

Approximate nutritional analysis per serving:
Calories 196, Protein 8 g, Carbohydrates 35 g, Fat 4 g, Cholesterol 9 mg, Sodium 119 mg

Main Courses

MEATLESS SHEPHERD'S PIE

½ cup (120 ml) uncooked lentils
2 cups (480 ml) water
1 bay leaf
3 cups (720 ml) boiling water
½ cup (120 ml) bulgur wheat
½ tsp (3 ml) garlic powder
¼ tsp (1 ml) sea salt
½ cup (120 ml) grated low-fat mozzarella cheese
1 medium onion, finely chopped
16-oz can (480 g) tomatoes, drained
1½ cups (355 ml) potato flakes
¼ tsp (1 ml) sea salt, optional

Cook lentils in 2 cups water with bay leaf about 15 minutes or until tender; drain. Remove bay leaf. While cooking lentils, pour 1 cup boiling water over bulgur wheat, garlic powder and salt; set aside for 10 minutes. Preheat oven to 350°F (180°C). Layer in oiled 8x8-inch oven dish in the following order: bulgur wheat, lentils, mozzarella cheese, onion and tomatoes. Mix potato flakes, 2 cups boiling water and salt and layer on top of tomatoes. Bake for 30 minutes. Serves 4.

Approximate nutritional analysis per serving:
Calories 276, Protein 16 g, Carbohydrates 48 g, Fat 4 g, Cholesterol 8 mg, Sodium 284 mg

CHILE RELLEÑO CASSEROLE

1 lb (455 g) soft tofu, rinsed
2 7-oz cans (420 g) diced green chiles
1 cup (240 ml) shredded Monterey Jack cheese
6 egg whites plus 2 eggs
⅔ cup (160 ml) nonfat milk
1 cup (240 ml) all-purpose flour
1 tsp (5 ml) baking powder
½ tsp (3 ml) ground cumin
1 cup (240 ml) shredded cheddar cheese
28-oz can (840 ml) chunky tomato sauce
¼ cup (60 ml) chopped fresh cilantro

Coarsely mash tofu; drain in colander 10 minutes. Combine tofu, diced green chiles and Monterey Jack cheese and spread on bottom of lightly greased 12x8-inch baking dish. In large bowl of electric mixer whip egg whites and whole eggs on high speed until thick and foamy. Add milk, flour, baking powder and cumin; beat until smooth. Pour egg mixture over chiles; sprinkle with cheddar cheese.

Bake, uncovered, at 375°F (190°C) for 25-30 minutes or until golden brown. Meanwhile heat tomato sauce in medium saucepan over low heat until hot through. Stir in cilantro; serve immediately with casserole. Serves 6.

Approximate nutritional analysis per serving:
Calories 340, Protein 22 g, Carbohydrates 30 g, Fat 14 g, Cholesterol 85 mg, Sodium 620 mg

TEMPEH ÉTOUFFÉE

12-oz pkg (360 g) soy or multigrain tempeh, cubed
2 cups (480 ml) chopped fresh tomatoes, with juice,
*   or 16 oz (480 g) canned stewed tomatoes*
¼ tsp (1 ml) dry mustard or 1 tsp (5 ml) prepared mustard
2 tsp (10 ml) hot pepper sauce or 1 tsp (5 ml) cayenne pepper
1 bunch green onion, chopped
1 green bell pepper, chopped
1 yellow onion, chopped
2 cloves garlic, minced
½-¾ cup (120-180 ml) water
2 tsp (10 ml) dried thyme
1 tbsp (15 ml) dried basil
2 tbsp (30 ml) dried parsley
2 tbsp (30 ml) soy sauce
2 tbsp (30 ml) lemon juice
2 tbsp (30 ml) flour

Place everything, except the flour, in a pot; bring to a boil. Stir in the flour. Simmer for 30 minutes. Serve over rice. Serves 4.

Approximate nutritional analysis per serving w/o rice:
Calories 355, Protein 24 g, Carbohydrates 50 g, Fat 8 g, Cholesterol 0 mg, Sodium 588 mg

TEMPEH CURRY

1 small onion, chopped
1 tbsp (15 ml) oil
12-oz pkg (360 g) soy or multigrain tempeh, cubed
1 cup (240 ml) water
¼ cup (60 ml) soy sauce
2 tbsp (30 ml) flour
2 tsp (10 ml) curry powder
1 tsp (5 ml) marjoram
1 large tomato peeled and chopped
10-oz can (300 g) pineapple chunks, drained
1 cup (240 ml) cooked peas

In large pot sauté onion in oil on medium-high heat until onion is transparent. Add tempeh, water, soy sauce, flour, curry powder and marjoram. Bring to simmer and stir until thickened. Add tomato, pineapple and peas. Serve over rice or noodles. Serves 4.

Approximate nutritional analysis per serving w/o rice:
Calories 419, Protein 24 g, Carbohydrates 57 g, Fat 12 g, Cholesterol 0 mg, Sodium 36 mg

SEA BASS WITH TOMATO & DILL RELISH

2 cups (480 ml) diced tomatoes
½ cup (120 ml) diced red onion
½ cup (120 ml) diced cucumber
¼ cup (60 ml) chopped fresh dill
½ cup (120 ml) seasoned rice vinegar
2 tbsp (30 ml) fresh lemon juice
2 tbsp (30 ml) hazelnut oil or salad oil
freshly ground white pepper
4 small new potatoes, boiled, with skins on
1 lb (455 g) sea bass or halibut steak

Toss all ingredients except bass in salad bowl, adding pepper to taste, and leave to blend in refrigerator for at least 1 hour. Meanwhile grill or broil fish. Serve relish over fish. Serves 4.

Approximate nutritional analysis per serving:
Calories 301, Protein 25 g, Carbohydrates 32 g, Fat 9 g, Cholesterol 60 mg, Sodium 113 mg

MOROCCAN-STYLE SALMON

1 small onion, sliced
2 garlic cloves, minced
1 tbsp (15 ml) olive oil
28-oz can (840 g) whole tomatoes, peeled, coarsely chopped
*   and liquid reserved*
4 tsp (20 ml) honey
1 tsp (5 ml) grated fresh lemon peel
¾ tsp (4 ml) ground cumin
1½ tsp (8 ml) lemon juice
cayenne pepper
24-36 oz (720-1080 g) salmon fillet
2 tbsp (30 ml) chopped toasted almonds
2 tbsp (30 ml) chopped cilantro
3 cups (720 ml) cooked couscous or rice

Sauté onion and garlic in olive oil in medium skillet over medium-high heat until golden. Stir in tomatoes, tomato liquid, honey, lemon peel and cumin. Simmer 10-15 minutes. Stir in lemon juice and season with salt, pepper and cayenne to taste. Meanwhile season salmon fillets with salt and pepper. Broil 4-6 inches from heat, allowing 10 minutes per inch of thickness, measured at thickest part. Place each fillet on dinner plate. Top with tomato sauce; sprinkle with almonds and cilantro. Serve with couscous. Serves 4.

Approximate nutritional analysis per serving:
Calories 525, Protein 42 g, Carbohydrates 50 g, Fat 17 g, Cholesterol 94 mg, Sodium 440 mg

BAKED DILLED SALMON ON RICE

olive oil cooking spray
1 medium onion, chopped
3 cloves garlic, minced
3 medium tomatoes, diced
½ lb (230 g) mushrooms, sliced
3 tbsp (45 ml) lemon juice
3 tbsp (45 ml) chopped fresh dill
2 cups (480 ml) cooked brown rice
4 6-oz (720 g) salmon fillets

Coat nonstick skillet with olive oil cooking spray. Sauté onion, garlic, tomatoes and mushrooms for 5 minutes or until softened. Add lemon juice and fresh dill. Remove from heat. Add salt and pepper to taste. Spray baking dish with olive oil spray. Spread rice evenly over bottom. Top rice with salmon. Cover each filet with vegetable mixture. Cover pan with foil. Bake for 20 minutes at 350°F (180°C). Serves 4.

Approximate nutritional analysis per serving:
Calories 405, Protein 42 g, Carbohydrates 34 g, Fat 12 g, Cholesterol 65 mg, Sodium 230 mg

GRILLED AHI WITH MANGO-PEACH SALSA

¼ cup (60 ml) mint leaves
¼ cup (60 ml) cilantro
¼ cup (60 ml) chopped red onion
4 tbsp (60 ml) lime juice
2 tbsp (30 ml) fresh ground ginger
1 tbsp (15 ml) minced serrano chile
1 cup (240 ml) mango-peach juice
1 large ripe mango
4 6-oz (720 g) Ahi tuna steaks

Mix all ingredients together except for the mango and tuna. Marinate the fish overnight in half the mixture. Heat coals in grill. Peel and cut the mango into cubes; add to the other half of the marinade. Grill the tuna steaks 6-8 minutes, turning once. Spoon the mango salsa over the fish and serve at once. Serves 4.

Approximate nutritional analysis per serving:
Calories 383, Protein 52 g, Carbohydrates 18 g, Fat 11 g, Cholesterol 83 mg, Sodium 99 mg

SWEET & SOUR FISH

1 cup (240 ml) julienned carrots
½ cup (120 ml) thinly sliced celery
½ cup (120 ml) thinly sliced onion
2 tsp (10 ml) vegetable oil
½ cup (120 ml) orange juice
¼ cup (60 ml) honey
1 tsp (5 ml) grated fresh gingerroot
½ tsp (3 ml) salt
pinch black pepper
pinch cayenne pepper
1½ lbs (683 g) halibut steak or snapper fillet

Stir-fry vegetables in oil in medium skillet until tender-crisp.

Add orange juice, honey and seasonings; bring mixture to boil. Arrange fish in 13x9x2-inch oiled baking pan. Spoon vegetable mixture over fish. Bake covered at 425°F (220°C), allowing 10 minutes per inch of thickness of fish or until fish flakes when tested with fork. Serves 4.

Approximate nutritional analysis per serving:
Calories 307, Protein 36 g, Carbohydrates 26 g, Fat 6 g, Cholesterol 54 mg, Sodium 383 mg

SESAME CHICKEN WITH
MANGO SWEET & SOUR SAUCE

MANGO SWEET & SOUR SAUCE:
2 tbsp (30 ml) sesame oil
1 tsp (5 ml) minced garlic
1 tsp (5 ml) minced ginger
4 tbsp (60 ml) mango vinegar
4 tbsp (60 ml) honey
1 tbsp (15 ml) tamari sauce
1 tsp (5 ml) arrowroot

SESAME CHICKEN:
4 tsp (20 ml) canola oil
4 boneless, skinless free-range chicken breasts
1 bunch green onion, cut into 1-inch pieces
1 large ripe mango, peeled and cut into 1-inch cubes
freshly ground pepper
2 tsp (10 ml) sesame seeds

Mango Sweet & Sour Sauce: Heat the sesame oil in a 10-inch skillet over medium heat. Add the garlic and ginger and sauté for 30 seconds. Add the vinegar, honey and tamari sauce. Bring to a boil and stir constantly for 30 seconds more. Remove from the heat and transfer to a small container. Reserve. Yields ½ cup.

Sesame Chicken: Rinse out the pan and return it to the heat. Add the canola oil. When the oil is hot, add the chicken breasts and sauté gently, about 4 minutes. Turn the chicken breasts and add the green onion. Continue to cook for 2 minutes longer and then add the mango. Continue to cook until the chicken is done. Toss the mango and the onion during this time until they are cooked through. Remove from the heat and pour off any excess fat from the pan. Combine the arrowroot with the cooled sweet and sour sauce. Pour the sauce over the chicken and return it to the heat for several minutes.

Remove from the heat and arrange the chicken, mango and onion equally among four plates. Cover each breast with the remaining sauce, season with pepper and sprinkle with sesame seeds. Serve immediately. Serves 4.

Approximate nutritional analysis per serving:
Calories 384, Protein 28 g, Carbohydrates 34 g, Fat 16 g, Cholesterol 72 mg, Sodium 324 mg

RATATOUILLE-TOPPED CHICKEN

1 tbsp (15 ml) olive oil
1 medium onion, chopped
2 cloves garlic, minced
½ red bell pepper, chopped
½ green bell pepper, chopped
1 small eggplant, cubed
14-oz can (420 g) chopped tomatoes
1 yellow squash, sliced
1 zucchini, sliced
2 tbsp (30 ml) chopped fresh oregano
4 boneless, skinless chicken breasts
olive oil cooking spray
½ lb (230 g) pasta, cooked and drained

Coat nonstick skillet with olive oil. Add onion, garlic, peppers and eggplant. Sauté 10 minutes until soft. Add the next four ingredients and pepper to taste. Cover and simmer for 15 minutes. Preheat oven to 350°F (180°C). While sauce is simmering, brown chicken breasts in skillet sprayed with olive oil cooking spray, about 3 minutes on each side. Place in baking dish, set aside and keep warm. Cover chicken with sauce, cover with foil and bake 15 minutes. Serve over pasta. Serves 4.

Vegetarian Variation: Omit chicken and serve over rice or pasta.

Approximate nutritional analysis per serving w/ chicken:
Calories 478, Protein 37 g, Carbohydrates 64 g, Fat 9 g, Cholesterol 66 mg, Sodium 241 mg

Approximate nutritional analysis per serving w/o chicken:
Calories 337, Protein 11 g, Carbohydrates 64 g, Fat 5 g, Cholesterol 0 mg, Sodium 180 mg

ROSEMARY-LEMON CHICKEN

1 lb (455 g) baby red potatoes
1 lb (455 g) carrots
4 skinless chicken breasts
½ cup (120 ml) lemon juice
1 tsp (5 ml) finely grated lemon peel
2 tbsp (30 ml) honey
2 tbsp (30 ml) vegetable oil
2 tbsp (30 ml) chopped fresh rosemary leaves

Parboil potatoes and carrots about 5 minutes. Rinse in cool water, drain and set aside. Marinate chicken in rest of ingredients for 30 minutes to several hours. Cover and bake at 375°F (190°C) for 30 minutes. Remove cover, add potatoes and carrots and bake for another 20 minutes. Serves 4.

Approximate nutritional analysis per serving:
Calories 412, Protein 30 g, Carbohydrates 50 g, Fat 11 g, Cholesterol 66 mg, Sodium 116 mg

ARUGULA-STUFFED CHICKEN ROLLS

4 boneless chicken breasts
1 bunch fresh arugula, heavy stems removed
freshly ground black pepper
2 tbsp (30 ml) butter or margarine
½ cup (120 ml) chicken broth
½ cup (120 ml) dry white wine
½ lb (230 g) mushrooms, sliced
4 green onions, sliced

Lay chicken breasts skin side down. Pound each to an even ½-inch thickness. Divide arugula into four portions and place one portion on each breast. Roll breast jelly-roll-style and secure with toothpicks. Season with pepper. Sauté in 1 tbsp butter until golden brown, about 4 minutes. Add broth, wine, mushrooms and green onions. Reduce heat, cover and simmer until meat is no longer pink inside, about 10-12 minutes.

   Transfer chicken to warm platter and keep warm. Bring cooking liquid, mushrooms and green onions to boil until reduced by half. Add 1 tbsp butter and stir until butter is melted. Pour sauce over chicken. Serves 4.

Approximate nutritional analysis per serving:
Calories 224, Protein 29 g, Carbohydrates 4 g, Fat 8 g, Cholesterol 84 mg, Sodium 238 mg

PACIFIC CHICKEN, SHRIMP & KIWI FRUIT KEBABS

LIME-GINGER MARINADE:
6 tbsp (90 ml) lime juice
3 tbsp (45 ml) honey
2 tbsp (30 ml) rice vinegar
2 tbsp (30 ml) olive oil
1½ tsp (8 ml) chopped cilantro
1 tsp (5 ml) grated fresh gingerroot
¼ tsp (1 ml) red hot pepper flakes

½ lb (230 g) boneless, skinless chicken breasts
     cut into 16 1-inch pieces
1 large red bell pepper, cored and cut into 16 pieces
1 small red onion, cut into 16 pieces
6 whole kiwi fruits, peeled and quartered
16 peeled frozen shrimp

Lime-Ginger Marinade: Whisk together ingredients until well combined.

   Toss chicken, pepper and onion with marinade; marinate 1-2 hours in refrigerator. When ready to cook, toss kiwi fruit and shrimp with other ingredients to coat with marinade. Divide ingredients among eight skewers. Grill or broil 3-4 minutes per side, turning skewers once, until chicken and shrimp are cooked through. Serves 4.

Note: If using wooden skewers, soak in water for 15 minutes prior to assembling meat and vegetables.

Approximate nutritional analysis per serving:
Calories 294, Protein 20 g, Carbohydrates 38 g, Fat 8 g, Cholesterol 80 mg, Sodium 99 mg

MOROCCAN CHICKEN TAJINE

8 skinless chicken thighs
¼ cup (60 ml) honey
1 large onion, chopped
3 cloves garlic, minced
2 cinnamon sticks, 3 inches each
juice of 1 lemon
2 tsp (10 ml) turmeric
½ cup (120 ml) dried apricots, quartered

Arrange chicken thighs in bottom of Dutch oven. Pour honey over chicken; sprinkle with onion and then with minced garlic. Add cinnamon sticks and sprinkle with lemon juice and turmeric. Top with apricot quarters and bake at 350°F (180°C) for about 1 hour or until fork can be inserted in chicken with ease. Remove cinnamon sticks from chicken mixture and serve with rice or couscous. Serves 4.

Approximate nutritional analysis per serving w/o rice:
Calories 290, Protein 29 g, Carbohydrates 33 g, Fat 6 g, Cholesterol 115 mg, Sodium 123 mg

ITALIAN CHICKEN & RICE

cooking oil spray
2 whole chicken breasts, deboned and cut into slices
½ lb (230 g) zucchini, thinly sliced
½ cup (120 ml) chopped green onion
16-oz can (480 g) tomatoes, chopped and liquid reserved
3 cups (720 ml) cooked light brown rice
¼ cup (60 ml) chopped parsley
½ tsp (3 ml) salt
¼ tsp (1 ml) pepper
pinch oregano

Coat large skillet with cooking oil spray. Sauté chicken until lightly browned. Add zucchini; cook until tender-crisp. Stir in remaining ingredients. Cover, reduce heat and simmer 15 minutes or until heated through. Serves 4.

Approximate nutritional analysis per serving:
Calories 409, Protein 18 g, Carbohydrates 77 g, Fat 3 g, Cholesterol 23 mg, Sodium 335 mg

ARTICHOKE CHICKEN

2 tbsp (30 ml) butter
1½ cups (360 g) sliced mushrooms
13¾-oz can (413 ml) chicken broth
16-oz jar (480 g) marinated artichoke hearts, juice reserved
3 boneless, skinless chicken breasts, split
1 cup (240 ml) nonfat plain yogurt

In a medium frying pan melt the butter. Add the mushrooms and sauté until wilted.

In a large skillet mix the chicken broth with the juice from the artichoke hearts; bring to a boil. Add the chicken, cover and poach for 20 minutes, turning the chicken occasionally. Remove the chicken from the pan and place it in a covered dish to keep it warm. Reduce the liquid in the pan by half. Add the artichoke hearts and mushrooms and stir. Reduce the heat and add the yogurt, mixing gently. Pour over the warm chicken. Serve with rice pilaf. Serves 6.

Approximate nutritional analysis per serving w/o rice:
Calories 162, Protein 19 g, Carbohydrates 14 g, Fat 4 g, Cholesterol 35 mg, Sodium 429 mg

MICROWAVE STIR-FRY WITH CHICKEN

1 tbsp (15 ml) oil
1 tbsp (15 ml) butter
3 medium onions, quartered
1 green pepper, cut into ¼-inch strips
3 cups (720 ml) thinly sliced cabbage
1 cup (240 ml) diagonally sliced carrots
¼ cup (60 ml) sliced green onion
1 cup (240 ml) cauliflower florets
1 cup (240 ml) broccoli florets
3 stalks celery, sliced diagonally
10-oz pkg (300 g) frozen pea pods
½ cup (120 ml) cooked chicken pieces
½ cup (120 ml) sliced mushrooms

Put oil, butter and quartered onions into 3-quart casserole. Microwave uncovered on high for 3 minutes until hot. Mix in pepper, cabbage, carrots, green onion, cauliflower, broccoli, celery and pea pods. Microwave covered on high for 4 minutes. Add chicken and mushrooms. Microwave uncovered on high for 4-6 minutes more. Serves 6.

Approximate nutritional analysis per serving:
Calories 126, Protein 7 g, Carbohydrates 16 g, Fat 5 g, Cholesterol 13 mg, Sodium 57 mg

INCREDIBLE LOW-FAT CHICKEN POT PIE

4-5 lb (1.8-2.3 kg) chicken

PASTRY CUTOUTS:
1 cup (240 ml) flour
1 tsp (5 ml) sugar
½ tsp (3 ml) salt
4 tbsp (60 ml) unsalted butter, softened
3 tbsp (45 ml) low-calorie sour cream
1½ tsp water

1 lb (455 g) fresh pearl onions
1 lb (455 g) carrots, cut into ½-inch chunks
1 lb (455 g) fresh asparagus
1 tsp (5 ml) olive oil
1 tsp (5 ml) butter
½ lb (230 g) yellow finn potatoes, peeled and thinly sliced
1 lb (455 g) celery root, peeled and thinly sliced
1 cup (240 ml) peeled and thinly sliced parsnips
2 leeks, white only, thinly sliced
2 garlic cloves
1 sprig fresh thyme
¾ cup water
3 cups (720 ml) chicken stock
1 lb (455 g) fresh peas

Roast chicken until done, about 1 hour. Allow to cool.

Pastry Cutouts: Place flour in large bowl or on work surface. Spoon sugar and salt over it. Cut butter into flour until mixture is texture of cornmeal. Spoon sour cream and 1½ tsp water over top. Mix with fork to incorporate sour cream. Using your hands form dough into ball. Refrigerate 1 hour before rolling out. Roll dough and cut into desired shapes. Place on baking sheet. Freeze for 15 minutes. Bake 10-12 minutes at 425°F (220°C).

While chicken is cooking and dough is resting in refrigerator, bring large pot of water to boil. Cook pearl onions 5-7 minutes. Drain and run under cold water. When cool enough, peel and set aside. Cook carrots in boiling water until tender-crisp. Cook asparagus likewise 3 minutes and drain.

To make sauce, combine olive oil, butter, potatoes, celery root, parsnips, leeks, garlic, thyme and ¾ cup water. Cover and simmer until water is almost evaporated, about 15-20 minutes. Add chicken stock and bring to simmer. Cook covered until vegetables are very tender. Discard thyme. Transfer to food processor or blender. Process until smooth. Season with salt and pepper. Remove meat from chicken and discard skin and bones.

Combine chicken and vegetable sauce and add peas; transfer to casserole. Bake 30 minutes or until bubbly. Take out of oven and arrange pastry cutouts over top. Serves 10.

Approximate nutritional analysis per serving:
Calories 451, Protein 47 g, Carbohydrates 37 g, Fat 13 g, Cholesterol 142 mg, Sodium 705 mg

GREEK ISLAND CHICKEN

4 skinless chicken breast halves
2 tbsp (30 ml) olive oil
1 onion, chopped
3 cloves garlic, minced
1 red bell pepper, cut into strips
1 cup (240 ml) dried tomato halves
1½ cups (355 ml) dry white wine
⅓ cup (80 ml) sliced, pitted black olives
1 lemon, sliced
1½ tsp (8 ml) cinnamon
1 tsp (5 ml) honey
½ tsp (3 ml) pepper
dried parsley, chopped, for garnish

In large skillet cook chicken breasts in olive oil over medium heat for about 5 minutes, turning once. Add onion, garlic and red pepper. Cook, stirring often, about 4 minutes or until onions are limp. With kitchen shears halve tomato pieces; stir into skillet with remaining ingredients except parsley. Salt to taste. Cover and simmer 15 minutes. Remove cover and cook 5 more minutes or until chicken is tender and sauce is slightly reduced. Sprinkle with chopped parsley. Serve over rice pilaf if desired. Serves 4.

Approximate nutritional analysis per serving:
Calories 323, Protein 30 g, Carbohydrates 16 g, Fat 10 g, Cholesterol 68 mg, Sodium 444 mg

GINGER TURKEY STIR-FRY

2 cups (480 ml) boiling water
1 cup (240 ml) cracked bulgur wheat
⅓ cup (80 ml) water
2 tbsp (30 ml) fresh lemon juice
2 tbsp (30 ml) honey
1 tsp (5 ml) grated fresh gingerroot
1 tbsp (15 ml) low-sodium soy sauce
1 large clove minced garlic
2 tbsp (30 ml) cornstarch
1 tbsp (15 ml) vegetable oil
2 cups (480 ml) diagonally sliced carrots
2 cups (480 ml) broccoli florets
2 cups (480 ml) sliced mushrooms
8-oz can (240 g) sliced water chestnuts
1 lb (455 g) turkey breast cutlets, cut into ½x2-inch strips

Pour 2 cups boiling water over cracked wheat and let stand 1 hour; drain.

Combine ⅓ cup water, lemon juice, honey, ginger, soy sauce and garlic. Dissolve cornstarch in mixture; set aside.

Heat oil over high heat in wok or large skillet. Add carrots; stir-fry 3 minutes or until tender-crisp. Add broccoli, mushrooms and water chestnuts; stir-fry about 2 more minutes. Remove from pan.

Stir-fry turkey until lightly browned. Add sauce and cook, stirring constantly, until thickened and translucent. Add vegetables; heat throughout. Serve over cracked wheat. Serves 4.

Approximate nutritional analysis per serving:
Calories 315, Protein 29 g, Carbohydrates 44 g, Fat 4 g, Cholesterol 63 mg, Sodium 160 mg

STUFFED PEPPERS

4 medium green peppers
olive oil cooking spray
¾ lb (360 g) lean ground turkey
1 medium onion, chopped
2 cloves garlic, minced
½-1 tsp (3-5 ml) black pepper
2 tbsp (30 ml) chopped fresh tarragon
2 cups (480 ml) cooked rice
8-oz can (240 ml) tomato sauce
4 tbsp (60 ml) grated Parmesan cheese

VEGETARIAN VARIATION:
2 cups (480 ml) canned black beans, rinsed and drained

Cut off pepper tops and remove seeds. Chop tops, discarding stems. Set aside. Bring large saucepan of water to boil. Immerse peppers; boil 5 minutes. Drain and set aside. Spray large, nonstick fry pan with olive oil spray and sauté chopped pepper tops, turkey, onion, garlic, black pepper and tarragon until turkey is browned. Add rice and all but 4 tbsp of tomato sauce. Mix well. Fill peppers with mixture. Place in baking dish. Top with 4 tbsp tomato sauce and Parmesan cheese. Serves 4.

   Vegetarian Variation: Omit turkey and add beans.

Approximate nutritional analysis per serving w/turkey:
Calories 358, Protein 24 g, Carbohydrates 41 g, Fat 11 g, Cholesterol 61 mg, Sodium 168 mg

Approximate nutritional analysis per vegetarian serving :
Calories 336, Protein 15 g, Carbohydrates 65 g, Fat 3 g, Cholesterol 4 mg, Sodium 332 mg

TURKEY MEATBALLS WITH LEMON SAUCE

1 cup (240 ml) cooked kasha, any granulation
3 cups (720 ml) chicken or turkey broth
1 egg, beaten
1 tsp (5 ml) Worcestershire sauce
1 tsp (5 ml) grated lemon peel
1½ lbs (683 g) ground raw turkey
2 tbsp (30 ml) cooking oil
¼ cup (60 ml) low-fat plain yogurt
1 tbsp (15 ml) cornstarch
1 tbsp (15 ml) lemon juice
1 small carrot, finely shredded
1 green onion, diced

Prepare kasha according to package directions, using 2 cups chicken broth. In mixing bowl combine prepared kasha with next four ingredients; blend well. Shape into 12 balls. In large skillet heat oil and brown turkey meatballs on all sides. Add 1 cup broth; cover and simmer 20 minutes. Use slotted spoon to transfer turkey meatballs to serving dish. In small bowl combine yogurt, cornstarch and lemon juice. Combine with pan juices in skillet and cook until sauce is thick and bubbly. Add carrot and onion. Pour sauce over turkey meatballs. Serves 4.

Approximate nutritional analysis per serving:
Calories 166, Protein 17 g, Carbohydrates 5 g, Fat 6 g, Cholesterol 74 mg, Sodium 141 mg

SPICED BEEF WITH
BLACK BEANS & PLANTAINS

4 tbsp (60 ml) vegetable oil
2 lbs (910 g) boneless chuck steak, cut into ½-inch cubes
2 14½-oz cans (870 ml) low-sodium beef broth
1 bay leaf
1½ cups (355 ml) chopped onion
¼ tsp (1 ml) pepper
1 fresh Anaheim chile, seeded and finely chopped
1-2 fresh or rehydrated dried serrano, jalapeño or pasilla chiles
½ clove elephant garlic, minced, or 4 cloves garlic, minced
2 ripe yellow or black plantains, peeled and chopped
1 cup diced tomatoes
2 tsp (10 ml) capers
11-oz pkg (330 g) black beans, cooked and drained
2-oz jar (60 g) chopped pimientos, drained
3 cups (720 ml) hot cooked rice

Heat 2 tbsp vegetable oil in large Dutch oven; add chuck steak. Brown meat on all sides; drain off fat. Add broth, bay leaf, half the onion and pepper. Bring to boil; reduce heat. Cover and simmer 1-1½ hours or until meat is very tender. Transfer meat to plate with slotted spoon, reserving juices; cover.

Measure 1½ cups juices (add water if necessary). In large skillet heat 1 tbsp oil. Add chiles, remaining onion and garlic; sauté 2 minutes. Add 1 tbsp more oil and plantains; sauté 5 minutes. Stir in measured juices, tomatoes and capers. Bring to boil; reduce heat and simmer, covered, for 15 minutes. Add meat and cooked black beans to chile mixture and cook until heated through. Season to taste. Spoon mixture into serving dish; sprinkle on pimiento. Serve over hot cooked rice. Serves 6.

Approximate nutritional analysis per serving:
Calories 474, Protein 68 g, Carbohydrates 73 g, Fat 24 g, Cholesterol 153 mg, Sodium 320 mg

BLACK BEAN CHILE CON CARNE

2 tbsp (30 ml) vegetable oil
1 lb (455 g) lean ground beef, pork or turkey
¾ cup (180 ml) chopped red or yellow onion
¾ cup (180 ml) chopped carrots
1 cup (240 ml) chopped green or red bell pepper
1 clove elephant garlic, peeled and minced
28-oz can (840 g) diced tomatoes, with juice reserved
2 14½-oz cans (870 ml) low-sodium beef broth
1 bay leaf
1-2 fresh or rehydrated dried chipotle, jalapeño,
*   serrano, yellow or Anaheim chiles*
½ tsp (3 ml) salt
¼ tsp (1 ml) ground cumin
1 cup (240 ml) niblet corn
11-oz pkg (330 g) black beans, cooked and drained

In Dutch oven heat oil. Sauté beef until browned. Drain, reserving 2 tbsp drippings in pan. Sauté onion, carrots, bell pepper and garlic until tender; drain off excess fat. Add tomatoes and their juices, broth, browned meat, bay leaf, chiles, salt and cumin. Bring to boiling; reduce heat. Simmer 30 minutes. Stir in corn and black beans; simmer 5 minutes more or until chile is desired consistency. Serve with shredded cheese, diced avocado, chopped onion, hot corn or flour tortillas or tortilla chips as accompaniments. Yields 10 cups.

Approximate nutritional analysis per serving w/o accompaniments:
Calories 316, Protein 24 g, Carbohydrates 29 g, Fat 12 g, Cholesterol 45 mg, Sodium 388 mg

BURGUNDY BEEF STEW

2 lbs (910 g) lean beef stew meat, cubed
2 tbsp (30 ml) low-sodium soy sauce
6 carrots, cut into chunks
2 cups (480 ml) red or white rose potatoes, peeled and cut into chunks
2 large onions, sliced
2 stalks celery, diced
2 cloves garlic, minced
¼ tsp (1 ml) black pepper
1 cup (240 ml) dry red wine
1 cup (240 ml) quartered mushrooms
1 tbsp (15 ml) minced fresh marjoram
1 tsp (5 ml) minced fresh thyme

Place beef in large covered casserole dish and stir in soy sauce. Add carrots, potatoes, onions, celery, garlic, pepper and wine. Cover and bake at 325°F (165°C) for 1½ hours. Add mushrooms, stir gently, cover and bake 1 hour longer. Stir in marjoram and thyme and bake for 15 minutes. Flour or cornstarch may be added to thicken sauce. Serves 6.

Approximate nutritional analysis per serving:
Calories 355, Protein 40 g, Carbohydrates 28 g, Fat 6 g, Cholesterol 98 mg, Sodium 323 mg

LAMB CHOPS WITH HERB-YOGURT MARINADE

MARINADE:
1 tbsp (15 ml) each dried basil, rosemary and oregano
1 tbsp (15 ml) chopped fresh garlic
1 cup (180 ml) nonfat plain yogurt
1 tbsp (15 ml) Worcestershire sauce
pinch freshly ground black pepper

4 lean loin lamb chops, trimmed of fat
2 cups (480 ml) cooked spinach

Mix marinade ingredients together in glass or ceramic bowl. Add lamb chops and coat well. Cover and refrigerate overnight.

Prepare barbecue. When grill is medium-hot, remove lamb chops from marinade, keeping well coated. Grill over medium heat for 5 minutes per side for medium-rare. Serve ½ cup spinach with each chop. Serves 4.

Approximate nutritional analysis per serving:
Calories 184, Protein 23 g, Carbohydrates 10 g, Fat 6 g, Cholesterol 58 mg, Sodium 194 mg

LAMB KEBABS WITH MINT

½ cup (120 ml) chopped fresh mint
1 cup (240 ml) low-fat plain yogurt
2 tbsp (30 ml) Dijon mustard
3 cloves garlic, minced
2 tbsp (30 ml) lemon juice
14 oz (420 g) boneless leg of lamb, cubed
4 plum tomatoes, halved
4 small zucchini, cut into 1-inch chunks
2 cups (480 ml) cooked couscous or brown rice

Mix mint, yogurt, mustard, garlic, lemon juice and salt and pepper to taste in medium bowl. Add lamb pieces and refrigerate overnight. Preheat broiler or barbecue. Thread lamb with tomatoes and zucchini onto skewers, reserving marinade. Place under hot broiler or on hot grill. Cook about 8-10 minutes for medium or until desired doneness, turning and basting with marinade. Serve over couscous or brown rice. Serves 4.

Note: If using wooden skewers, soak in water for 15 minutes prior to assembly.

Approximate nutritional analysis per serving:
Calories 395, Protein 38 g, Carbohydrates 36 g, Fat 11 g, Cholesterol 95 mg, Sodium 227 mg

MOROCCAN COUSCOUS

Lamb Stew

1 tbsp (15 ml) olive oil
1 lb (455 g) lean boneless lamb, cut into 1-inch cubes
1 medium onion, sliced
1½ cups (355 ml) chicken broth or water
1 cup (240 ml) sliced carrots
1 cup (240 ml) diced tomatoes
1 tsp (5 ml) ground cinnamon
½ tsp (3 ml) ground coriander
¼ tsp (1 ml) cayenne pepper
¼ tsp (1 ml) pepper
¼ tsp (1 ml) saffron, optional
11-oz pkg (330 g) garbanzo beans or 15-oz can (450 g) garbanzo beans,
*   rinsed and drained*
3 cups (720 ml) chopped or shredded cabbage
1 cup (240 ml) cubed zucchini or yellow summer squash
6-oz pkg (180 g) couscous
2 cups (480 ml) water
⅔ cup (160 ml) raisins

In Dutch oven heat oil; sauté lamb and onion until browned. Stir in broth, carrots, tomatoes and seasonings. Bring to boil; reduce heat. Simmer, covered, for 1 hour. Stir in garbanzo beans, cabbage and zucchini; simmer 30 minutes more. Meanwhile in 1-quart saucepan combine couscous, water and raisins. Bring to boil; reduce heat. Simmer 5 minutes. Fluff couscous with fork. Serve lamb stew over couscous. Serves 4.

Approximate nutritional analysis per serving:
Calories 577, Protein 59 g, Carbohydrates 97 g, Fat 19 g, Cholesterol 122 mg, Sodium 130 mg

SEITAN IRISH STEW

2 cups (480 ml) diced seitan
1 cup (240 ml) rutabagas, peeled and cut into ½-inch cubes
1 cup (240 ml) onion, cut into ½-inch cubes
1 cup (240 ml) carrots, washed, not peeled, and diced or roll cut
1 cup (240 ml) potatoes, peeled and cut into ½-inch cubes
2 bay leaves
½ tsp (3 ml) rosemary
½ tsp (3 ml) chopped fresh garlic
½ tsp (3 ml) basil
1 tbsp (15 ml) chopped fresh parsley
4 tsp (20 ml) sesame oil or oil of choice
2 cups (480 ml) plus 4 tbsp (60 ml) water
5 tsp (25 ml) tamari sauce
½ cup (120 ml) chopped celery
4-5 tbsp (60-75 ml) arrowroot

Place first 11 ingredients in 2-quart saucepan. Sauté on medium heat for about 8 minutes, stirring occasionally to prevent burning. Add 2 cups water and tamari and bring mixture to simmer. Cook for another 10 minutes or until vegetables are tender-crisp. Add celery at end of cooking process to help retain color.

In separate bowl mix 4 tbsp water and arrowroot well. Turn heat off under stew and vigorously stir in arrowroot mixture. Turn heat on to medium and stir constantly until mixture thickens. Serves 4.

Approximate nutritional analysis per serving:
Calories 284, Protein 21 g, Carbohydrates 38 g, Fat 6 g, Cholesterol 0 mg, Sodium 708 mg

Vegetables

PEAS, PEARLS & CARROTS MEDLEY

11 oz (330 g) frozen green peas
1 bunch baby carrots, peeled and trimmed,
   or 1 cup (240 ml) half-slices of carrots
10 oz (300 g) fresh pearl onions
1 tbsp (15 ml) butter or margarine
1 tbsp (15 ml) chopped fresh basil or 1 tsp (5 ml) crushed dried basil
2 tsp (10 ml) chopped fresh thyme or dill
   or ½ tsp (3 ml) crushed dried thyme or dill

Cook green peas according to package directions. Add baby carrots to peas during last 8 minutes of cooking. Boil pearl onions in their skins for 3-5 minutes or until nearly tender. Drain onions and rinse well in cold water. Slice off stem ends and slip off skins. Halve any large onions. Drain peas and carrots; place in serving bowl with onions. In saucepan melt butter; stir in herbs. Drizzle over vegetables; sprinkle with salt and pepper. Toss well and serve. Serves 6.

Approximate nutritional analysis per serving:
Calories 83, Protein 3 g, Carbohydrates 13 g, Fat 2 g, Cholesterol 0 mg, Sodium 74 mg

PEPERONATA OF EGGPLANT
WITH FRESH THYME

1 cup (240 ml) diced eggplant
1 cup (240 ml) sliced onion
2 tbsp (30 ml) olive oil
1 tbsp (15 ml) chopped fresh garlic
1 cup (240 ml) diced red bell peppers
2 cups (480 ml) diced Roma tomatoes
8 pitted kalamata or niçoise olives
2 tbsp (30 ml) chopped fresh thyme
freshly ground black pepper
8 oz (240 g) pasta

Lightly salt the eggplant and place it on a paper towel to drain.

In a thick-bottomed saucepan cook the onion in the olive oil until light brown. Add the garlic and eggplant and cook for 5 minutes. Add the bell pepper and tomatoes and cook for 10 minutes. Take off the stove and add the olives, thyme and black pepper. Cook the pasta and serve it with the peperonata over it. Serves 4.

Variation: Peperonata may also be served cold or at room temperature, inside an omelet, on top of grilled bread or just by itself with crusty bread.

Approximate nutritional analysis per serving:
Calories 311, Protein 9 g, Carbohydrates 48 g, Fat 10 g, Cholesterol 49 mg, Sodium 77 mg

TAMARILLO RATATOUILLE

1½ cups (355 ml) chicken broth
1 small eggplant, peeled and diced
4 tamarillos, any variety, peeled and diced
1½ cups (355 ml) sliced mushrooms
1 red, golden or orange bell pepper, chopped
1 clove elephant garlic, minced, or 3 cloves regular garlic, minced
2 tbsp (30 ml) chopped fresh basil
1 tbsp (15 ml) chopped fresh oregano
2 tbsp (30 ml) grated Parmesan cheese

In large saucepan or Dutch oven combine broth, eggplant, tamarillos, mushrooms, bell pepper, garlic, basil and oregano. Bring mixture to boil; reduce heat. Simmer, partially covered, for 30 minutes or until vegetables are tender. Season with salt and pepper to taste; serve topped with Parmesan cheese. Serves 6.

Approximate nutritional analysis per serving:
Calories 59, Protein 3 g, Carbohydrates 10 g, Fat 1 g, Cholesterol 2 mg, Sodium 52 mg

PURÉED BUTTERNUT SQUASH

4 lbs (1.8 kg) butternut squash
1 large onion, chopped
1 clove garlic, peeled and diced
2 cloves shallots, peeled and diced
12 sliced black olives
2 tbsp (30 ml) sweet butter
¼ cup (60 ml) light cream
¼ tsp (1 ml) nutmeg
3 twists freshly ground pepper

Peel the squash and cut it into even-size slices. Remove the seeds. Steam until tender in the basket of a double boiler, about 15 minutes. Sauté the onion, garlic, shallots and olives in the butter. Process the squash in a food processor. Add the onion, garlic, shallots, olives and butter to the squash in the food processor. Add the cream and flavor with nutmeg and pepper. Process until the squash is puréed. Serve hot. Serves 8.

Approximate nutritional analysis per serving:
Calories 161, Protein 3 g, Carbohydrates 28 g, Fat 6 g, Cholesterol 16 mg, Sodium 73 mg

SQUASH-N-APPLE SAUTÉ

2 medium squash
2 tbsp (30 ml) butter or margarine
2 large Jonathan or Delicious apples, cored and chopped
1 leek, sliced, white part only
2 tbsp (30 l) white or rosé wine
¼ tsp (1 ml) ground cinnamon
pinch ground black pepper
pinch ground allspice

Halve each squash; cook halves covered in small amount of boiling water for 15 minutes. Meanwhile in large skillet melt butter. Add apples and leek slices and sauté for 5 minutes. Add wine and seasonings and cook 3 minutes more. Reserving shells, scoop out squash and mash; blend with apple mixture in skillet. Spoon mixture back into squash shells and serve immediately. Serves 4.

Approximate nutritional analysis per serving:
Calories 220, Protein 3 g, Carbohydrates 43 g, Fat 6 g, Cholesterol 16 mg, Sodium 71 mg

SPAGHETTI SQUASH

1 spaghetti squash
1 tbsp (15 ml) olive oil
2 garlic cloves, finely chopped
fresh basil leaves, shredded
¾ cup (180 ml) chopped plum tomatoes

Preheat oven to 375° F (190° C). Cut open squash, discard seeds and remove long vibrant-yellow strings of squash meat that look like pasta. Toss squash strings with olive oil, garlic, basil and tomatoes. Bake, covered, until tender, approximately 30-45 minutes. Serves 4.

Approximate nutritional analysis per serving:
Calories 85, Protein 2 g, Carbohydrates 12 g, Fat 4 g, Cholesterol 0 mg, Sodium 30 mg

EXOTIC-STYLE GRILLED VEGETABLES

2 lbs (910 g) squash, halved and seeded
1 lb (455 g) baby red or small yellow finn potatoes
1 Japanese eggplant, stem removed and halved lengthwise
½ lb (230 g) baby carrots, trimmed and peeled
1 lb (455 g) plantains, peel on and quartered
leaves of 1 cactus, thorns removed and cut into 1-inch strips
6 oz (180 g) pearl onions, peeled
6 oz (180 g) fresh shiitake or whole oyster mushrooms, stems removed

BASTING SAUCE:
¼ cup (60 ml) olive or vegetable oil
¼ cup (60 ml) lime juice
2 cloves garlic, minced
2 tbsp (30 ml) minced fresh mint
1 tbsp (15 ml) minced fresh oregano
¼ tsp (1 ml) salt
¼ tsp (1 ml) pepper

chopped fresh mint, for garnish
fresh oregano leaves, for garnish

Precook squash, potatoes, eggplant, baby carrots, plantains, cactus leaves and pearl onions until not quite tender.

Meanwhile mix oil, lime juice, garlic, herbs and seasonings for basting sauce until well combined.

Drain vegetables well; arrange on grill over medium-hot heat or on lightly oiled broiler pan from preheated broiler. Brush mushrooms and vegetables liberally with basting sauce and turn once. Remove vegetables from grill and peel plantains. Spoon remaining sauce over vegetables to serve. Garnish with chopped mint and oregano. Serves 4.

Note: Small shiitake or oyster mushrooms and pearl onions can be threaded on skewers for easier handling and to prevent accidental "fall-throughs" on grill. If using wooden skewers, soak in water for 15 minutes before assembling.

Approximate nutritional analysis per serving:
Calories 530, Protein 11 g, Carbohydrates 100 g, Fat 16 g, Cholesterol 0 mg, Sodium 273 mg

MEXICAN VEGETABLE SAUTÉ

2 tbsp (30 ml) vegetable oil
½ cup (120 ml) chopped onion
1-2 cloves elephant garlic, peeled, halved and thinly sliced
1-2 fresh or rehydrated dried jalapeño, serrano, chipotle, Fresno,
*   Anaheim or yellow chiles, seeded and cut into thin strips*
1½ cups (355 ml) diced cooked potatoes or yams
*   or peeled, diced uncooked plantains*
1½ cups (355 ml) diced zucchini or chayote squash
½ cup (120 ml) whole kernel corn
1 tbsp (15 ml) chopped fresh cilantro

Heat oil in large skillet; sauté onion, garlic and chiles over medium-low heat for 3-5 minutes or until garlic is tender; do not allow vegetables to burn. Add potatoes and squash; sauté 5-10 minutes more or until squash is tender. Add corn and cilantro; season with salt and pepper to taste. Cook until warmed through. Serves 5.

Approximate nutritional analysis per serving:
Calories 141, Protein 3 g, Carbohydrates 21 g, Fat 6 g, Cholesterol 0 mg, Sodium 59 mg

GRILLED SUMMER VEGETABLES

3 tbsp (45 ml) olive oil
3 tbsp (45 ml) basil vinegar
2 Japanese eggplants, halved lengthwise
2 zucchini, halved lengthwise
2 yellow squash, halved lengthwise
4 slices red onion, ½ inch thick
1 sweet red pepper, quartered and seeded

Whisk oil into vinegar. Brush vegetables with vinaigrette. Prepare barbecue at medium-high heat. Grill vegetables until tender, about 4 minutes per side. Serves 8.

Approximate nutritional analysis per serving:
Calories 73, Protein 1 g, Carbohydrates 6 g, Fat 5 g, Cholesterol 0 mg, Sodium 3 mg

SAUTÉED PLANTAINS & SWEET POTATOES

4 tbsp (60 ml) butter or margarine
2 tbsp (30 ml) cooking oil
2 cups (480 ml) sliced cooked sweet potatoes or yams
2 plantains, peeled and chopped
½ cup (120 ml) chopped green onion
½ cup (120 ml) chopped cooked ham, optional
1 clove garlic, minced
½ cup (120 ml) chicken or beef broth
1-2 tbsp (15-30 ml) chopped fresh thyme, chervil, dill or savory

In large skillet heat 2 tbsp butter and cooking oil. Add potatoes, plantains, onion, ham and garlic. Cook, stirring frequently, about 5 minutes. Add broth; cover and simmer 10 minutes or until plantains are tender. Add remaining butter and herbs; season to taste with salt and pepper. Serves 6.

Approximate nutritional analysis per serving:
Calories 275, Protein 3 g, Carbohydrates 41 g, Fat 13 g, Cholesterol 21 mg, Sodium 156 mg

POTATOES WITH SHALLOT-GARLIC-ONION RELISH

8 oz (240 g) pearl onions, peeled,
    or 1 cup (240 ml) chopped yellow onion
6 shallots, peeled and thinly sliced
1 clove elephant garlic, peeled and finely minced
1 cup (240 ml) beef or chicken broth
2 tbsp (30 ml) chopped fresh parsley
¼ tsp (1 ml) pepper
1½ lbs (683 g) small potatoes, sliced ¼ inch thick

Halve peeled pearl onions. Place in medium saucepan with shallots, garlic and broth. Bring to boil; reduce heat to simmer. Cover and braise 5 minutes or until vegetables are very tender. Uncover and simmer 5-10 minutes more or until nearly all liquid has disappeared. Stir in parsley and pepper; set aside.

Cook potatoes in boiling water to cover for 10-15 minutes. Drain well; serve hot with relish Serves 4.

Approximate nutritional analysis per serving:
Calories 204, Protein 6 g, Carbohydrates 45 g, Fat .7 g, Cholesterol 0 mg, Sodium 168 mg

MASHED-POTATO BOATS

5 large potatoes
¾ cup (180 ml) soy powder
onion powder, to taste
garlic powder, to taste
½ cup (120 ml) chopped onions
½ cup (120 ml) chopped red bell pepper
½ cup (120 ml) diced celery
3 tbsp (45 ml) canola oil
margarine or butter, optional
½ cup (120 ml) nutritional yeast, optional
paprika

Bake potatoes at 350°F (180°C) until soft. Scoop potato pulp into bowl, leaving skins intact for boats. Mash pulp. Add soy powder, onion powder, garlic powder and salt to taste. If too stiff, add water.

Sauté chopped onion, bell pepper and celery in canola oil. Add onion mixture to mashed potatoes. Add margarine to taste and yeast. Place mashed mixture back into skins; sprinkle with paprika. Reheat if necessary, covered, in hot oven until piping hot. Serve with main dish and green or orange vegetable. Serves 5.

Approximate nutritional analysis per serving:
Calories 441, Protein 11 g, Carbohydrates 73 g, Fat 12 g, Cholesterol 0 mg, Sodium 153 mg

BROCCOLI & MUSHROOM-STUFFED POTATOES

4 large russet potatoes
1 cup (240 ml) trimmed, chopped broccoli
1 cup (240 ml) sliced mushrooms
olive oil or vegetable spray
8-oz container (240 g) low-fat cottage cheese
3 tbsp (45 ml) low-fat milk
fresh chives, chopped

Bake potatoes at 350°F (180°C) until soft. Cut tops off potatoes and let cool for 10 minutes. In medium frying pan sauté broccoli and mushrooms in olive oil spray until soft. Scoop out potatoes, leaving shells intact. Mash potatoes with cottage cheese and milk to desired consistency; add salt and pepper to taste. Add fresh chives, broccoli and mushrooms to potato mixture. Fill potato shells with mixture. Potatoes may be made ahead to this point. If so, cover and chill. Bring to room temperature before baking. Bake for 30 minutes at 350°F (180°C). Serves 4.

Approximate nutritional analysis per serving:
Calories 272, Protein 14 g, Carbohydrates 51 g, Fat 2 g, Cholesterol 6 mg, Sodium 257 mg

STUFFED SQUASH

4 buttercup or acorn squash
1 large apple, chopped
⅓ cup (80 ml) chopped walnuts
¼ cup (60 ml) sugar
¼ cup (60 ml) raisins
2 tbsp (30 ml) butter or margarine
¼ cup (60 ml) maple syrup

Preheat oven to 400°F (205°C). Wash squash. Cut tops off and scrape out seeds and strings. Place cut side down on baking sheet and bake until squash is tender when pricked with fork. Combine remaining ingredients in saucepan and heat gently until well blended and soft. When squash is done, remove from oven and fill cavities with filling. Pour some maple syrup over each just to moisten tops and return to oven to heat through. Serves 8.

Approximate nutritional analysis per serving:
Calories 248, Protein 4 g, Carbohydrates 50 g, Fat 6 g, Cholesterol 8 mg, Sodium 39 mg

SCALLOPED POTATOES

6 cups (1.4 l) water
6 medium potatoes, pared and cut into ¼-inch slices
¾ cup (180 ml) chopped onion
½ cup (120 ml) diced green pepper
2 tbsp (30 ml) margarine
4 tbsp (60 ml) flour
2 cups (480 ml) soy milk
1½ cups (355 ml) shredded cheddar cheese alternative
¼ cup (60 ml) pimientos
¼ tsp (1 ml) garlic powder

Bring water to boil; add potatoes, onion and green pepper. As soon as water resumes boiling, re-move from heat and drain vegetables. Turn into greased 7½x12-inch baking dish. Melt margarine in medium-size pan; stir in flour until well mixed. Gradually stir in soy milk and cook over low heat, stirring until mixture thickens and begins to boil. Remove from heat and stir in 1 cup shredded cheese alternative, pimientos, garlic powder and salt and pepper to taste. Pour over potatoes and stir gently to combine. Sprinkle remaining cheese alternative over top. Bake, uncovered, at 350°F (180°C) for 35-40 minutes or until potatoes are tender and sauce is bubbly around edges. Serves 8.

Approximate nutritional analysis per serving:
Calories 230, Protein 10 g, Carbohydrates 36 g, Fat 6 g, Cholesterol 0 mg, Sodium 380 mg

SPAGHETTI SQUASH-STUFFED PEPPERS

¼ cup (60 ml) low-salt chicken broth
1 cup (240 ml) chopped zucchini, yellow crookneck, pattypan,
*   scallopini or sunburst squash*
½ cup (120 ml) chopped shiitake mushrooms
¼ cup (60 ml) sliced green onion
1 tbsp (15 ml) chopped fresh basil or 1 tsp (5 ml) crushed dried basil
1 tbsp (15 ml) chopped fresh thyme or 1 tsp (5 ml) crushed dried thyme
1 clove garlic, minced
¼ tsp (1 ml) black pepper
1½ cups (355 ml) spaghetti squash, cooked, seeded and
*   fluffed into strands*
4 sweet bell peppers, any color
¼ cup (60 ml) shredded nonfat or low-fat Swiss or cheddar cheese

In skillet heat broth to simmering. Add chopped squash, mushrooms, onion, herbs, garlic and black pepper. Simmer, uncovered, stirring occasionally, for 4 minutes or until vegetables are tender. Remove from heat. Stir in cooked spaghetti squash. Slice tops off bell peppers and discard seeds. Spoon filling into peppers; sprinkle on shredded cheese. Add tops. Place in shallow baking dish sprayed with aerosol cooking spray. Cover and bake in 375°F (190°C) oven for 30-35 minutes or until heated through. Serves 4.

Approximate nutritional analysis per serving:
Calories 73, Protein 4 g, Carbohydrates 13 g, Fat 2 g, Cholesterol 2 mg, Sodium 17 mg

TABOULI-STUFFED PEPPERS

1 pkg tabouli
8-oz can (240 ml) tomato sauce
½ cup (120 ml) chopped parsley
¼ cup (60 ml) chopped black olives
4 large red or green bell peppers
olive rounds, for garnish

Prepare tabouli according to package directions, omitting tomatoes. After liquids have been absorbed, add tomato sauce, parsley and chopped olives. Cut peppers in half vertically, removing seeds but leaving stems intact. Steam, open side down, for 5 minutes. Stuff peppers with tabouli. Garnish with olive rounds. Place in large baking dish and cover with aluminum foil. Bake at 375°F (190°C) for 20-25 minutes. Serves 8.

Approximate nutritional analysis per serving:
Calories 113, Protein 4 g, Carbohydrates 24 g, Fat 4 g, Cholesterol 0 mg, Sodium 547 mg

ZESTY STUFFED PEPPER POTS

4 large green bell peppers
1 tbsp (15 ml) safflower oil
1 cup (240 ml) diced celery
½ cup (120 ml) diced onion
1 medium jalapeño pepper, seeded and minced
1 cup (240 ml) garbanzo beans, cooked and mashed
1 cup (240 ml) canned crushed tomatoes
1 tbsp (15 ml) minced basil leaves
½ tsp (3 ml) garlic powder or 2 cloves fresh garlic
¼ tsp (1 ml) black pepper
4 tbsp (60 ml) low-fat plain yogurt

Cut tops from peppers and remove seeds. Remove stems, leaving hole in center of each top. Parboil peppers and tops for 3 minutes, drain and set aside. In large skillet heat oil and sauté celery and onion for 3 minutes. Remove from heat and add ½ of minced jalapeño along with garbanzo beans, tomatoes, basil, garlic powder and black pepper. Combine well and stuff peppers with the mixture. Combine remaining jalapeño with yogurt and spoon 1 tbsp on top of each pepper. Cover with pepper tops and place peppers in nonstick baking pan. Bake at 350°F (180°C) for 40-45 minutes. Serves 4.

Approximate nutritional analysis per serving:
Calories 152, Protein 6 g, Carbohydrates 23 g, Fat 5 g, Cholesterol .3 mg, Sodium 172 mg

BULGUR-STUFFED SQUASH

½ large squash
1 tbsp (15 ml) cooking oil
1 clove garlic, minced
½ cup (120 ml) chopped walnuts or pecans
2 cups (480 ml) cooked bulgur or rice
2 shallots, chopped, optional
1 large tomato, chopped
¼ cup (60 ml) water or chicken broth
1½ tsp (8 ml) chopped fresh rosemary
  or ½ tsp (3 ml) crushed dried rosemary
1½ tsp (8 ml) chopped fresh oregano
  or ½ tsp (3 ml) crushed dried oregano
1½ tsp (8 ml) chopped fresh basil
  or ½ tsp (3 ml) crushed dried basil
¾ cup (180 ml) shredded Swiss, Monterey Jack or mozzarella cheese

Parboil squash in small amount of water in Dutch oven or large saucepan for about 20 minutes. Drain; scoop out and discard seeds. Scoop out flesh, leaving ½-inch shell. Chop squash or separate into strands if using spaghetti squash. Set aside.

In large skillet heat oil; add garlic and walnuts. Sauté 2 minutes over medium heat. Add cooked bulgur, shallots, tomato and water. Stir until well blended; cook 3 minutes. Add herbs; blend well. Taste mixture; season with salt and pepper if desired. Add squash pieces; mix well.

Place squash shell, cut side up, in baking pan with small amount of water in bottom of pan. Spoon filling mixture into shell. Cover with foil. Bake in 375°F (190°C) oven for 20 minutes. Uncover; sprinkle shredded cheese on top. Bake 10 minutes more or until hot and cheese is bubbly. Serve immediately. Serves 3.

Approximate nutritional analysis per serving:
Calories 556, Protein 26 g, Carbohydrates 67 g, Fat 26 g, Cholesterol 25 mg, Sodium 110 mg

VEGETABLES, RICE & CHEESE PLATTER

1 tbsp (15 ml) cooking oil
1 medium onion, sliced
2 medium carrots, julienned
2 medium yellow squash or zucchini, halved lengthwise
  and thinly sliced
1 ripe tomato, seeded and chopped
1 cup (240 ml) sliced fresh mushrooms
11-oz pkg (330 g) black-eyed peas, cooked
2 cups (480 ml) wild, brown or white rice, cooked
½ cup (120 ml) low-sodium chicken or beef broth
1 tbsp (15 ml) chopped fresh savory or basil
  or 1 tsp (5 ml) crushed dried savory or basil
½ tsp (3 ml) salt
¼ tsp (1 ml) pepper
½ cup (120 ml) shredded sharp cheddar cheese
½ cup (120 ml) shredded Monterey Jack or mozzarella cheese

In large skillet heat oil; sauté onion and carrots for 5-8 minutes or until tender. Add squash, tomato and mushrooms; cover and cook 3 minutes more. Drain peas; stir into skillet with rice, broth, savory, salt and pepper. Cook, covered, for a few minutes to heat. Sprinkle cheeses over top; cover skillet until cheese melts. Serve at once. Serves 5 as main dish.

Approximate nutritional analysis per serving:
Calories 448, Protein 23 g, Carbohydrates 66 g, Fat 11 g, Cholesterol 22 mg, Sodium 380 mg

SQUASH & MILLET CASSEROLE

2 medium zucchini squash
2 medium yellow crookneck squash
1½-2 tsp (8-10 ml) herb salt
1 bell pepper, chopped
1 large onion, chopped
½ lb (230 g) grated cheese, optional
1½ cups (355 ml) raw millet
2 1-lb cans (910 g) stewed tomatoes with juice

Preheat oven to 350°F (180°C). Generously oil 2-quart casserole dish. Chop all squash into ½-inch-thick slices. Sprinkle with herb salt and pepper to taste. Toss all remaining ingredients with squash until well mixed. Cover very tightly and bake 1 hour or until squash is tender and millet is puffed and tender. Serves 4.

Approximate nutritional analysis per serving:
Calories 283, Protein 11 g, Carbohydrates 66 g, Fat 2 g, Cholesterol 0 mg, Sodium 583 mg

LAYERED ROOT VEGETABLE STEW

1 piece wakame (sea vegetable), soaked and diced
1 cup (240 ml) spring water
1 onion, cut into segments
2 tbsp (30 ml) tamari sauce
1 turnip, cut into segments
1 small rutabaga, cut into small pieces
1 daikon radish, diagonally cut
1 scallion, thinly sliced
1 carrot, sliced
1 piece burdock, thinly sliced
1 lotus root, thinly sliced

Place wakame and water in pot. Turn up flame until water boils; reduce to medium flame. Begin by layering onion over wakame. Sprinkle a little tamari on onion and then layer turnip. Sprinkle a little tamari on turnip and continue to layer and sprinkle rest of roots in the order they are listed. Cover pot and simmer for 50 minutes. Gently stir and serve over rice or as side dish. Serves 4.

Approximate nutritional analysis per serving:
Calories 162, Protein 4 g, Carbohydrates 38 g, Fat .5 g, Cholesterol 0 mg, Sodium 671 mg

VEGETABLE & HERB CURRY

1 box vegetable–brown-rice mix
½ medium onion, thinly sliced
2 stalks celery, chopped
1 green bell pepper, chopped
2 tbsp (30 ml) vegetable oil
1 fresh apple, chopped, or ½ cup (120 ml) dried apple, chopped
¼ cup (60 ml) raisins
¼ cup (60 ml) water
2 tsp (10 ml) curry powder
salt or tamari sauce

Cook rice according to package directions. While rice is cooking, sauté vegetables in oil until barely tender, 3-5 minutes. Stir in apple, raisins and water. Cover and steam for a few minutes until raisins are softened. When rice is done, add rice and curry powder to vegetables. Stir gently until well mixed. Let sit a few minutes for flavors to mingle. Add salt or tamari to taste. Serves 6.

Approximate nutritional analysis per serving:
Calories 274, Protein 6 g, Carbohydrates 49 g, Fat 6 g, Cholesterol 0 mg, Sodium 214 mg

BEAN-VEGETABLE CASSEROLE WITH PESTO

½ cup (120 ml) diced onion
½ cup (120 ml) diced carrots
1 tbsp (15 ml) chopped fresh garlic
½ cup (120 ml) diced celery
1 tbsp (15 ml) olive oil
2 15-oz cans (900 g) low-sodium pinto, kidney, black,
  garbanzo or great northern beans, drained
1 cup (240 ml) quartered tomatoes
1 cup (240 ml) diced yellow or green squash

PESTO:
1 large fresh red bell pepper
½ tbsp (8 ml) chopped fresh garlic
2 tbsp (30 ml) fresh rosemary plus sprigs, for garnish
¼ cup (60 ml) fresh Italian parsley plus sprigs, for garnish
2 tbsp (30 ml) olive oil
¼ cup (60 ml) walnuts
¼ cup (60 ml) grated Parmesan cheese
fresh ground pepper

2 cups (480 ml) cooked rice

In a thick-bottomed saucepan sauté the onion, carrots, garlic and celery in the olive oil for 5 minutes. Add the beans and tomatoes and simmer for 5 minutes more. Add the squash and cook an additional 5 minutes.

Pesto: Seed the pepper. Place the pepper and garlic in a blender or food processor and purée. Remove the leaves from the rosemary. Add the herbs, pour in the oil and add the nuts, cheese and black pepper. Yields approximately 1 cup pesto.

To serve, place ½ cup of the rice into soup or pasta bowls and ladle the bean mixture over it. Top each serving with 1 tbsp of pesto and garnish with a sprig of rosemary or parsley. Serves 4.

Approximate nutritional analysis per serving:
Calories 369, Protein 16 g, Carbohydrates 61g, Fat 8 g, Cholesterol 1 mg, Sodium 71 mg

HONEYED RICE & VEGETABLE STIR-FRY

3 tbsp (45 ml) peanut oil
1 bunch green onions, bulbs and tops chopped separately
1 medium sweet potato, pared, halved lengthwise and thinly sliced
1 small green bell pepper, cut into thin strips
2 carrots, thinly sliced
1 zucchini, thinly sliced
2 cups (480 l) cooked brown rice
1 cup (240 ml) bean sprouts
1 cup (240 ml) fresh mushrooms, sliced
¼ cup (60 ml) honey
¼ cup (60 ml) tamari sauce

Heat oil in wok or large heavy skillet over medium-high heat.

Stir-fry onion bulbs, sweet potato, bell pepper, carrots and zucchini until barley tender. Add rice, sprouts, mushrooms and onion tops. Cook quickly; if necessary, add more oil. Combine honey and tamari sauce in cup. Pour over stir-fry mixture and stir. Serve immediately. Serves 6.

Approximate nutritional analysis per serving:
Calories 202, Protein 4 g, Carbohydrates 34 g, Fat 7 g, Cholesterol 0 mg, Sodium 604 mg

Condiments

CORN, JICAMA & PINEAPPLE SALSA

1½ cups (355 ml) peeled, finely chopped jicama
1 cup (240 ml) finely chopped fresh pineapple
1 cup (240 ml) whole kernel corn
½ cup (120 ml) diced green or red bell pepper
1 dried habañero chile, rehydrated and very finely chopped
2 tbsp (30 ml) chopped fresh cilantro
1 clove garlic, minced

In medium bowl combine jicama, pineapple, corn, bell pepper, habañero chile, cilantro and garlic. Process in two batches in food processor or blender, using a few stop-and-start motions for relishlike consistency. Cover and chill at least 1 hour to allow flavors to blend. Serve with fresh vegetable crudités or spoon over any steamed or cooked vegetable, barbecued meat, poultry, fish or scrambled eggs. Yields 3½ cups.

Approximate nutritional analysis per 1-tbsp serving:
Calories 6, Protein .2 g, Carbohydrates 1 g, Fat .1 g, Cholesterol 0 mg, Sodium 16 mg

SALSA WITH FRESH CILANTRO

¼ cup (60 ml) chopped fresh cilantro leaves
2 medium tomatoes, chopped
1 small green, serrano or jalapeño chile, peeled, seeded and minced
¼ cup (60 ml) chopped onion
1 clove garlic, minced
½ tsp (3 ml) red wine vinegar

Mix all ingredients. Serve with tortilla chips or other Mexican foods. Great in guacamole. Yields 1 cup.

Approximate nutritional analysis per 1-tbsp serving:
Calories 6, Protein .2 g, Carbohydrates 1 g, Fat .1 g, Cholesterol 0 mg, Sodium 55 mg

SALSA VARIATIONS

SALSA BASE:
3 cups (720 ml) chopped or diced tomatoes
2 cups (480 ml) chopped white onions
¾ cup (180 ml) chopped fresh cilantro

SALSA CARIBE:
2 cups (480 ml) diced ripe mango or papaya/nectarine combo
3 yellow wax chiles, chopped
juice of 1 lime
red Italian or sweet Spanish onion, optional
any hot yellow or red chile, optional
salt, optional

SALSA FRESCA:
2-3 jalapeño peppers, seeded, veined and chopped
juice of ½ lemon
green onion, optional
garlic, optional
serrano or Anaheim chiles, optional
salt, optional

BURNT SALSA:
2 roasted poblanos, seeded, veined and diced
4 roasted cloves garlic, chopped
juice of 1 lemon
1 tbsp (15 ml) fresh oregano
salt, optional
roasted tomatoes and onion, optional
chipotle peppers added to poblanos, optional

SALSA VERDE:
3 cups (720 ml) tomatillos
2-3 jalapeño peppers, chopped
serrano or Anaheim chiles, optional

Assemble salsa base and add ingredients for any of the variations. Improvise freely with optional ingredients. Chop by hand for coarser texture. Flavors will blend after standing for 1 hour. Salsa is best served fresh but will keep, refrigerated, for up to 3 days.

Salsa Caribe: Add mango, chiles and lime juice to salsa base. Yields 7½ cups.

Salsa Fresca: Add jalapeños and lemon juice to salsa base. Yields 5½ cups.

Burnt Salsa: Add poblanos, garlic, lemon juice and oregano to salsa base. Yields 5½ cups.

Salsa Verde: Substitute tomatillos for tomatoes in salsa base. Purée tomatillos and onion. Add jalapeños. Yields 5½ cups.

Approximate nutritional analysis per 1-tbsp serving salsa caribe:
Calories 3, Protein .1 g, Carbohydrates 1 g, Fat .03 g, Cholesterol 0 mg, Sodium 4 mg

Approximate nutritional analysis per 1-tbsp serving salsa fresca:
Calories 8, Protein .3 g, Carbohydrates .4 g, Fat .1 g, Cholesterol 0 mg, Sodium 10 mg

Approximate nutritional analysis per 1-tbsp serving burnt salsa:
Calories 8, Protein .3 g, Carbohydrates 2 g, Fat .1 g, Cholesterol 0 mg, Sodium 2 mg

Approximate nutritional analysis per 1-tbsp serving salsa verde:
Calories 8, Protein .3 g, Carbohydrates 2 g, Fat .1 g, Cholesterol 0 mg, Sodium 7 mg

HOMEMADE SALSA

6 fresh yellow chiles
6 fresh serrano or jalapeño chiles
2 green or red bell peppers
2 large red tomatoes, chopped
1 cup (240 ml) minced onion
2 cloves garlic, minced
3 tbsp (45 ml) lime juice
¼ tsp (1 ml) salt
½ tsp (3 ml) freshly ground black pepper

Preheat broiler. Pierce each chile and green pepper near stem with sharp knife. Arrange chiles and peppers on lightly greased baking sheet; roast, turning frequently with thongs, until all sides of chiles and peppers are blistered but not black. Remove from oven; place chiles and peppers in brown paper bag to soften skins. Let stand 15 minutes; slip skins off. Wear plastic gloves or cover fingers with plastic sandwich bags to prevent chile burn. Chop chiles and peppers. Discard seeds and veins if you prefer milder salsa. Stir together chopped chiles and peppers with remaining ingredients. Taste for seasoning. Store in tightly covered jar in refrigerator for up to 1 week or in freezer for 2-3 months. Yields 2 cups.

Approximate nutritional analysis per 1-tbsp serving:
Calories 13, Protein .5 g, Carbohydrates 3 g, Fat .1 g, Cholesterol 0 mg, Sodium 339 mg

MASTO-KHIAR RAITA

1 large or 2 small cucumbers
1 cup (240 ml) nonfat plain yogurt
2 tbsp (30 ml) honey
¼ cup (60 ml) raisins
½ cup (120 ml) chopped walnuts
1 small onion, grated, optional
1 tbsp (15 ml) crushed dried mint leaves

Peel and grate the cucumbers. Squeeze the cucumbers in a towel to remove excess liquid, then mix well with the yogurt and honey. Add the raisins, walnuts, onion, mint and salt and pepper to taste; mix well. Chill before serving with curry or cold meat. Yields 2½ cups.

Note: Up to 1 additional cup of yogurt can be added to taste.

Approximate nutritional analysis per ½-cup serving:
Calories 162, Protein 6 g, Carbohydrates 20 g, Fat 7 g, Cholesterol .8 mg, Sodium 40 mg

QUICK MANGO CHUTNEY

2 tbsp (30 ml) canola oil
1 medium yellow onion, minced
3 tbsp (45 ml) minced garlic
2 cups (480 ml) peeled and diced fresh mango
⅔ cup (160 ml) apple juice
5 tbsp (75 ml) mango vinegar
½ cup (120 ml) raisins
1 apple, peeled and diced
1 tbsp (15 ml) finely minced ginger
½ tsp (3 ml) allspice

Heat the oil over medium heat in a 2-quart saucepan. Add the onion and sauté 5 minutes. Add the garlic, mango, apple juice and vinegar. Simmer for 10 minutes, stirring often. Add the raisins, apple, ginger and allspice. Continue to simmer until the moisture has evaporated, about 10 more minutes. Refrigerate. Serve as a delicious condiment as an accompaniment to spicy foods or like a jam. Yields 3½ cups.

Approximate nutritional analysis per 2-tbsp serving:
Calories 45, Protein .3 g, Carbohydrates 9 g, Fat 1 g, Cholesterol 0 mg, Sodium 1 mg

CHUNKY GINGERED CRANBERRY SAUCE

1¼ cups (295 ml) apple cider or juice
3-oz pkg (90 g) dried cranberries
1 cup (240 ml) chopped dried apples or pears
⅓ cup (80 ml) raisins
1½ tsp (8 ml) minced fresh ginger

In a saucepan combine all ingredients. Bring to a boil; simmer, covered, 10 minutes. Remove from the heat; cool. Serve warm or chilled as a meat or poultry accompaniment or on sandwiches as a condiment. Yields 2 cups.

Approximate nutritional analysis per ¼-cup serving:
Calories 59, Protein .4 g, Carbohydrates 15 g, Fat .1 g, Cholesterol 0 mg, Sodium 6 mg

BEET-GARLIC RELISH

6-8 medium beets
1 cup (240 ml) champagne vinegar
½ cup (120 ml) water
½ cup (120 ml) sugar
4 whole black peppercorns
½ medium bay leaf
10 peeled cloves garlic
1 tbsp chopped fresh mint
3 tbsp (45 ml) minced shallots

Scrub the beets under cold running water until all dirt is removed. Simmer in lightly salted water until fork-tender, about 20-30 minutes. Remove from the water and allow to cool. Peel off the outer skin of the beets by rubbing them with paper towels. Combine the vinegar, water, sugar, black peppercorns and bay leaf and poach the garlic cloves in this mixture until tender. Remove from the heat and allow the garlic to cool in the poaching liquid. Slice the garlic thinly and dice the beets into ⅓-inch cubes. Toss the diced beets, poached garlic, chopped mint and minced shallots; season to taste with salt and black pepper. Adjust the acidity level with champagne vinegar or sugar if necessary. Serves 6.

Approximate nutritional analysis per serving:
Calories 98, Protein 1 g, Carbohydrates 24 g, Fat .1 g, Cholesterol 0 mg, Sodium 40 mg

YOGURT DIJON SALAD DRESSING

3 tbsp (45 ml) Dijon mustard
½ cup (120 ml) low-fat plain yogurt
½ tsp (3 ml) salt
pinch freshly ground pepper
3 tbsp (45 ml) lemon juice
1 tsp (5 ml) sugar
1 clove garlic, finely chopped
1 tbsp (15 ml) capers, drained

Combine the mustard, yogurt, salt, pepper, lemon juice, sugar and garlic in a small bowl; beat well. Stir in the capers and serve. Yields 1 cup.

Approximate nutritional analysis per 1-tbsp serving:
Calories 20, Protein <1 g, Carbohydrates 5 g, Fat <1 g, Cholesterol <1 mg, Sodium 149 mg

BERRY-POPPY SEED DRESSING

⅓ cup (80 ml) nonfat plain yogurt
2 tbsp (30 ml) raspberry or strawberry vinegar
1 tbsp (15 ml) maple syrup
½ tbsp (8 ml) poppy seeds

Mix all ingredients and serve over salad of red and green lettuce, oranges, avocado and kiwi. Yields ½ cup.

Approximate nutritional analysis per 1-tbsp serving:
Calories 26, Protein .7 g, Carbohydrates 3 g, Fat 1 g, Cholesterol .2 mg, Sodium 25 mg

THAI LIME, HERB & HONEY GLAZE

¼ cup (60 ml) lime juice
¼ cup (60 ml) Thai fish sauce
2 tbsp (30 ml) clover honey
2 tbsp (30 ml) rice vinegar
2 tsp (10 ml) minced green pepper
3 cloves fresh garlic, minced
2 tbsp (30 ml) water
2 scallions, minced
1 tsp (5 ml) chopped fresh thyme

Combine all liquid ingredients and blend well. Stir in remaining ingredients. Adjust all amounts and ingredients to taste. Best when used immediately. Yields approximately 1 cup.

Approximate nutritional analysis per ¼-cup serving:
Calories 56, Protein 4 g, Carbohydrates 10 g, Fat .2 g, Cholesterol 10 mg, Sodium 156 mg

YOGURT MARINADE

⅔ cup (160 ml) plain yogurt
juice and grated rind of ½ lemon
1 tsp (5 ml) mixed herbs
1 garlic clove, crushed

Mix together all ingredients. Spread the mixture over 2-2½ lb meat, fish or tempeh. Marinate for at least 1 hour before cooking as usual. Yields ¾ cup.

Approximate nutritional analysis per ¼-cup serving:
Calories 35, Protein 3 g, Carbohydrates 5 g, Fat .1 g, Cholesterol .9 mg, Sodium 43 mg

SECRET CHICKEN DIPPING SAUCE

16-oz can (480 ml) chicken broth
½ cup (120 ml) lemon juice
1 cup (240 ml) red wine vinegar
½ cup (120 ml) honey or brown sugar
½ cup (120 ml) barbecue sauce or ketchup

Combine all ingredients in saucepan and bring to boil. Use as dipping sauce for cooked chicken. Yields 4½ cups.

Approximate nutritional analysis per ½-cup serving:
Calories 73, Protein .8 g, Carbohydrates 19 g, Fat .3 g, Cholesterol 0 mg, Sodium 127 mg

HERBED HONEY-LIME SAUCE

½ cup (120 ml) minced onion
1 tbsp (15 ml) olive oil
1 cup (240 ml) dry white wine or chicken broth
¼ cup (60 ml) honey
¼ cup (60 ml) lime juice
2 tsp (10 ml) dry mustard
1 tsp (5 ml) minced fresh rosemary
½ tsp (3 ml) salt
dash pepper
1 tsp (5 ml) cornstarch
1 tsp (5 ml) water

Sauté onion in olive oil in medium saucepan over medium heat until onion is softened. Stir in wine, honey, lime juice, mustard, rosemary, salt and pepper; mix well and bring to boil. Combine cornstarch and water in small bowl or cup, mixing well. Add to sauce. Cook over low heat, stirring until sauce comes to boil and thickens. Serve over cooked turkey, chicken, fish or pork. Yields 2 cups.

Approximate nutritional analysis per ¼-cup serving:
Calories 78, Protein .4 g, Carbohydrates 11 g, Fat 2 g, Cholesterol 0 mg, Sodium 135 mg

LOW-FAT HOLLANDAISE SAUCE

10½-oz pkg (315 g) soft tofu, drained
4 tbsp (60 ml) nonfat plain yogurt
2 tbsp (30 ml) yellow mustard
1 tbsp plus 1 tsp (20 ml) white wine Worcestershire sauce
2 dashes white pepper
dash cayenne pepper
1 tbsp (15 ml) lemon juice
1 tbsp (15 ml) honey

In blender or food processor whip all ingredients until smooth and creamy. Heat sauce thoroughly and spoon immediately over cooked fresh asparagus or other fresh vegetable. Yields 1⅓ cup.

Approximate nutritional analysis per ⅓-cup serving:
Calories 74, Protein 5 g, Carbohydrates 8 g, Fat 2 g, Cholesterol 0 mg, Sodium 160 mg

HOMEMADE PASTA SAUCE

2 tbsp (30 ml) olive oil
1 cup (240 ml) chopped onion
½ cup (120 ml) chopped green bell pepper
2 cloves garlic, minced
28-oz can (840 g) whole peeled tomatoes, undrained
2 tbsp (30 ml) chopped fresh parsley
½ tsp (3 ml) crushed basil leaves
¼ tsp (1 ml) crushed oregano leaves
¼ tsp (1 ml) salt
pinch pepper

Heat oil in large saucepan over medium-low heat. Add onion, bell pepper and garlic; cook until tender. Stir in tomatoes, parsley, basil, oregano, salt and pepper. Crush tomatoes with spoon. Cook, uncovered, stirring often, until thickened, about 20-30 minutes. Serve immediately over hot cooked pasta or cool and freeze. Yields 2 cups.

Approximate nutritional analysis per ¼-cup serving:
Calories 60, Protein 1 g, Carbohydrates 6 g, Fat 3 g, Cholesterol 0 mg, Sodium 216 mg

Desserts

PEARS ELEGANZA

5 large pears, peeled but with stems on
2 cups (480 ml) water
½ cup (120 ml) sugar
1 cinnamon stick
1 inch fresh ginger, peeled
¾ cup (180 ml) plus 1 tbsp (15 ml) Grand Marnier
¾ cup (180 ml) heavy cream
1 tbsp (15 ml) confectioners sugar
1 cup (240 ml) nonfat plain yogurt
½ lb (230 g) carob chips

Core the pears from the bottom, keeping the stems in place and leaving walls about ½ inch thick. Reserve the cores. Place the pears upright in a large saucepan with the water, sugar, cinnamon stick, ginger and ½ cup Grand Marnier. Cook the pears until they are tender but not mushy–anywhere from 3-15 minutes, depending on the variety and ripeness. Cool, then add another ¼ cup Grand Marnier to the poaching liquid. Let stand in the refrigerator overnight.

Just before serving whip together ½ cup heavy cream, the confectioners sugar and 1 tbsp Grand Marnier in an electric mixer until stiff. On slow speed beat in ½ cup yogurt. Remove the pears from the liquid; fill the cavities of the pears with this semistiff mixture. Trim a ½-inch-thick piece from each reserved pear core and plug the pear cavities to keep the filling in place. To make the pears easy to eat, slice them horizontally at the point where the base narrows into the neck.

Melt the carob chips in a double boiler. Slowly add ¼ cup heavy cream and ½ cup yogurt, beating until smooth. Heat the sauce just until warmed through; do not allow it to simmer. Pour the sauce over the pears and serve. Any additional whipped cream mixture may be served separately on the side. Serves 5.

Note: The poaching liquid can be stored in the refrigerator and used to make this special dessert again.

Approximate nutritional analysis per serving:
Calories 756, Protein 7 g, Carbohydrates 92 g, Fat 29 g, Cholesterol 51 mg, Sodium 90 mg

FRUIT PARFAIT

24 strawberries
2 mangoes
¼ cup (60 ml) fresh orange juice
4 kiwis, peeled and sliced
12 raspberries

Put strawberries in blender. When puréed, pour into six parfait glasses or wide-bowl red wine glasses. Combine mangoes and orange juice in blender. Purée until smooth. Pour into parfait glasses on top of strawberries. Decorate with kiwi slices and raspberries. Place in refrigerator until ready to serve. Serves 6.

Approximate nutritional analysis per serving:
Calories 124, Protein 2 g, Carbohydrates 31 g, Fat 1 g, Cholesterol 0 mg, Sodium 5 mg

YOGURT CHEESE PARFAIT

1½ qts (1.4 l) nonfat plain yogurt, generously measured
1 cup (240 ml) sugar
1 tbsp (15 ml) finely grated lemon rind
2 cups (480 ml) fresh raspberries, blueberries or hulled,
    sliced strawberries

Four hours or the day before serving, stir the yogurt and sugar together. To make yogurt cheese line a colander with several layers of cheesecloth and place it over a bowl. Measure the yogurt mixture into the cheesecloth, cover and refrigerate. Let this mixture drain for 4 hours or overnight. The next day add the grated lemon rind to the yogurt cheese and mix well. If the yogurt cheese is too thick, it can be thinned slightly with additional yogurt. Spoon the yogurt cheese into parfait glasses, alternating with layers of fresh berries. Serves 4.

Approximate nutritional analysis per serving:
Calories 429, Protein 22 g, Carbohydrates 85 g, Fat 1 g, Cholesterol 7 mg, Sodium 281 mg

FRUIT COBBLER

1½ tbsp (25 ml) butter
1½ cups (355 ml) whole wheat flour
1 tsp (5 ml) non-alum baking powder
½ cup (120 ml) honey
1 egg, beaten
1 cup (240 ml) skim milk, soy milk or water
2 cups (480 ml) fresh fruit or canned fruit in natural juices

Melt butter in 9x9-inch pan or other baking dish of similar size. Mix flour, baking powder, honey, egg and milk. Pour mixture into butter. Add fruit on top of batter. Bake 30 minutes at 400°F (205°C). Serves 9.

Approximate nutritional analysis per serving:
Calories 170, Protein 4 g, Carbohydrates 37 g, Fat 2 g, Cholesterol 23 mg, Sodium 83 mg

FRESH FRUIT WITH CHOCOLATE-MINT SAUCE

1½ cups (355 ml) nonfat milk
2 tbsp (15 ml) low-fat margarine
½ cup (120 ml) unsweetened cocoa powder
½ cup (120 ml) sugar
1 tbsp (7 ml) finely chopped fresh mint leaves
1 tsp (5 ml) vanilla extract
4 cups (960 ml) fresh raspberries or sliced bananas

Scald milk in small saucepan. In separate saucepan melt margarine and add cocoa; stir well. Stir milk into cocoa mixture. Stirring with wire whisk, add sugar and mint; stir until sauce thickens, about 5 minutes. Add vanilla and remove from heat. Cool. Serve over ½ cup fresh raspberries per serving. Also delicious over frozen yogurt. Serves 8.

Approximate nutritional analysis per serving:
Calories 117, Protein 3 g, Carbohydrates 24 g, Fat 3 g, Cholesterol .8 mg, Sodium 59 mg

CRANBERRY-HONEY-PECAN CRUNCH PIE

2 cups (480 ml) fresh or frozen cranberries
1 cup (240 ml) fresh orange juice
½ cup (120 ml) honey
2 tbsp (30 ml) cornstarch
2 tbsp (30 ml) cold water
½ tsp (3 ml) orange extract
9-inch baked pie crust with fluted rim

TOPPING:
⅓ cup (80 ml) packed light brown sugar
3 tbsp (45 ml) honey
3 tbsp (45 ml) butter or margarine
1¾ cups (415 ml) pecan halves

In medium saucepan combine cranberries, juice and honey. Cook, uncovered, over low heat for 15 minutes if using fresh cranberries or for 20 minutes if using frozen berries. Cool. Purée cranberry mixture in blender; return to saucepan. Combine cornstarch and water in small bowl. Stir into cranberry mixture. Bring to boil and cook until thickened. Stir in orange extract. Cool; then pour into pie shell. Spoon prepared topping evenly over cranberry mixture. Bake at 350°F (180°C) for 20 minutes or until top is bubbly. Cool on wire rack. Serve at room temperature or chilled. Serves 10.

Topping: In medium saucepan combine brown sugar, honey and butter; cook, stirring 2 minutes or until mixture is smooth. Stir in pecan halves until well coated.

Approximate nutritional analysis per serving w/o topping:
Calories 173, Protein 1 g, Carbohydrates 29 g, Fat 6 g, Cholesterol 0 mg, Sodium 99 mg

Approximate nutritional analysis per serving w/topping:
Calories 380, Protein 3 g, Carbohydrates 43 g, Fat 24 g, Cholesterol 9 mg, Sodium 136 mg

YOGURT CREAM MOLD
WITH RASPBERRY SAUCE

YOGURT CREAM MOLD:
4 tsp (20 ml) unflavored gelatin
¼ cup (60 ml) cold water
1½ cups (355 ml) heavy cream
½ cup (120 ml) sugar
2¼ cups (540 ml) nonfat plain yogurt
1 tsp (5 ml) vanilla

RASPBERRY SAUCE:
2 10-oz pkgs (600 g) frozen raspberries in syrup, thawed
2 tbsp (30 ml) sugar
1 tbsp (15 ml) lemon juice
kiwi or orange slices, for garnish, optional

Yogurt Cream Mold: In a small bowl soften the gelatin in the cold water for about 10 minutes. In a saucepan combine the cream and sugar, then cook over medium heat, stirring constantly, for 5 minutes or until the sugar is dissolved. Remove from the heat.

Add the gelatin mixture and stir until the gelatin is dissolved. Transfer to a bowl. Let the mixture cool for about 5 minutes, then whisk in the yogurt and vanilla. Mix well.

Rinse a pretty 1-quart mold or individual molds with cold water; shake the mold but don't dry it. Pour in the yogurt mixture; chill for 2 hours.

Dip a knife in warm water and run the blade around the edge of the mold. Invert the mold and rap on it to loosen the yogurt cream.

Raspberry Sauce: Just before serving the mold, top with a sauce of combined raspberries, sugar and lemon juice. Garnish with kiwi slices. Serves 6.

Approximate nutritional analysis per serving:
Calories 446, Protein 10 g, Carbohydrates 54 g, Fat 22 g, Cholesterol 83 mg, Sodium 100 mg

RAISIN RICE PUDDING

⅓ cup (80 ml) turbinado sugar
2 tbsp (30 ml) cornstarch
pinch salt
2 cups (480 ml) skim milk
2 egg yolks
2 tbsp (30 ml) soft butter or 1 tbsp (15 ml) canola oil
2 tsp (10 ml) vanilla
2 cups (480 ml) cooked rice
1 tsp (5 ml) cinnamon
½ tsp (3 ml) nutmeg
1 cup (240 ml) seedless raisins

In saucepan combine sugar, cornstarch and salt. In separate bowl combine milk and egg yolks, then slowly stir into sugar mixture. Bring to boil over medium heat, stirring constantly. When boiling point is reached, stir 1 minute more or until mixture thickens. Remove from heat and add butter, vanilla, rice, spices and raisins. Mix well, cover, cool and chill. Serves 9.

Approximate nutritional analysis per serving:
Calories 191, Protein 4 g, Carbohydrates 39 g, Fat 3 g, Cholesterol 8 mg, Sodium 87 mg

PURPLE PUDDING

2½ cups (590 ml) grape juice or any other dark fruit juice
¾ cup (180 ml) blue cornmeal
1 cup (240 ml) nonfat plain yogurt
natural sweetener

Combine juice and blue cornmeal in saucepan and stir over low heat with wire whisk until very thick. Combine mixture with yogurt and sweetener and beat with electric mixer or in blender until creamy and smooth. Pour into small bowls and chill. Serves 8.

Approximate nutritional analysis per ½-cup serving:
Calories 114, Protein 3 g, Carbohydrates 24 g, Fat .7 g, Cholesterol .6 mg, Sodium 26 mg

KABOCHA-PUMPKIN CUSTARD

1 medium to large kabocha squash
½ tsp (3 ml) sea salt
1 tsp (5 ml) pumpkin pie spice
¼ cup (60 ml) kanten flakes
¾ cup (180 ml) spring water
½ cup (120 ml) maple syrup or brown rice syrup
2 tbsp (30 ml) kudzu
2 tbsp cold water
mint leaves, for garnish

Wash kabocha; cut away top and bottom stems and cut into pieces. Steam cut pieces with sea salt and ½ tsp pumpkin pie spice until soft. Meanwhile in saucepan dissolve kanten in spring water, cover and simmer for 5 minutes. Add syrup and remaining pumpkin pie spice and simmer for additional 5 minutes. Remove kabocha from steamer, scoop from skin and purée in food mill or blender. Add to kanten liquid and stir. Dissolve kudzu in cold water and add to pumpkin mixture, stirring constantly for 3-5 minutes on very low flame. Place in custard cups to set 1-2 hours. Garnish with mint leaves. Serves 4.

Approximate nutritional analysis per serving:
Calories 160, Protein 10 g, Carbohydrates 31 g, Fat .3 g, Cholesterol 0 mg, Sodium 293 mg

APPLE-RAISIN PUDDING

1 egg, beaten, plus 2 eggs
½ cup (120 ml) kasha, fine or medium granulation
¾ tsp (4 ml) salt
2 tbsp (30 ml) butter or margarine
1 cup (240 ml) water
¼ cup (60 ml) brown sugar, firmly packed
1 cup (240 ml) peeled and chopped tart apple
½ cup (120 ml) raisins
1 tsp (5 ml) grated lemon rind
1 tbsp (15 ml) lemon juice

Combine beaten egg, kasha and salt. In medium frying pan cook mixture in butter 3 minutes or until lightly toasted, stirring often. Stir in water; bring to boil. Cook, tightly covered, over low heat for 10 minutes. Remove from heat; cool, uncovered, about 15 minutes.

In medium bowl beat remaining 2 eggs with sugar. Stir in apple, raisins, lemon rind, lemon juice and kasha mixture. Pour into well-oiled 1½-quart casserole. Bake at 350°F (180°C) for 45 minutes or until center appears firm. Serve warm with whipped topping or your favorite lemon, orange or custard sauce. Serves 5.

Approximate nutritional analysis per serving:
Calories 247, Protein 6 g, Carbohydrates 40 g, Fat 8 g, Cholesterol 125 mg, Sodium 409 mg

FROZEN RASPBERRY-YOGURT CREAM

12-oz pkg (360 g) frozen unsweetened raspberries, thawed
¾ cup (180 ml) sugar
squeeze fresh lemon juice
2 cups (480 ml) nonfat plain yogurt
¾ cup (180 ml) heavy cream
2-3 tbsp (30-45 ml) raspberry liqueur, optional

Purée the thawed raspberries in a food processor, using the steel blade. Transfer to a sieve and press the mixture through the sieve into a bowl. Discard the seeds. Mix the sugar, lemon juice, yogurt, cream and raspberry liqueur into the raspberry juice. Place in the container of an ice cream maker and freeze according to the manufacturer's instructions. Serves 6.

This dessert can be eaten right away or transferred to a freezer container and stored in the freezer.

Approximate nutritional analysis per serving:
Calories 304, Protein 6 g, Carbohydrates 47 g, Fat 11 g, Cholesterol 42 mg, Sodium 74 mg

MANGO-CITRUS SORBET

SIMPLE SYRUP:
1 cup (240 ml) sugar
2 cups (480 ml) water

2 cups (480 ml) puréed mango
juice of 1 lemon
juice of 1 lime
1 egg white, lightly beaten

Simple Syrup: Cook sugar and water in saucepan over medium heat for 5-7 minutes to dissolve sugar. Chill syrup.

Put puréed mango into bowl. Add citrus juices and chilled syrup. Freeze in ice cream machine according to manufacturer's directions. Add beaten egg white halfway through freezing process. Yields 4 cups.

Approximate nutritional analysis per 1-cup serving:
Calories 265, Protein 1 g, Carbohydrates 68 g, Fat .3 g, Cholesterol 0 mg, Sodium 16 mg

CRANBERRY SORBET

1½ cups (355 ml) water
1½ cups (355 ml) sugar
1 lb (455 g) fresh cranberries
½ cup (120 ml) fresh orange juice
¼ cup (60 ml) fresh lemon juice
1 tbsp (15 ml) raspberry liqueur
1 egg white

Make a syrup by combining the water and sugar in a nonreactive saucepan and bringing it to a boil. Add the cranberries and orange juice and simmer until the berries burst from their skins, 25-30 minutes. Remove from the heat, purée in a food processor and strain through a fine sieve to remove the skins. Let cool. Then combine the cranberries, lemon juice and raspberry liqueur. Beat the egg white until stiff, blend into the purée and freeze. Serves 6.

Approximate nutritional analysis per serving:
Calories 126, Protein 1 g, Carbohydrates 31 g, Fat .2 g, Cholesterol 0 mg, Sodium 11 mg

MINT SORBET

1 cup (240 ml) water
3 oz (90 g) sugar
6 large sprigs flavored mint plus additional, for garnish
juice of 1 large lemon
1 egg white

Boil water and sugar together to dissolve sugar. Remove from heat and let stand 20 minutes with mint sprigs. Strain into rigid container, add lemon juice and leave to cool. Freeze until half-frozen; chop to loosen ice granules and fold in stiffly beaten egg white. Refreeze; rechop in 30 minutes if sorbet is too solid (versus granular). Decorate with mint sprigs. Serves 4.

Approximate nutritional analysis per serving:
Calories 90, Protein .9 g, Carbohydrates 23 g, Fat .02 g, Cholesterol 0 mg, Sodium 14 mg

HONEY-OAT BISCOTTI

½ *cup (120 ml) butter or margarine*
¾ *cup (180 ml) honey*
2 eggs
1 tsp (5 ml) vanilla
2 cups (480 ml) flour
3 tsp (15 ml) ground cinnamon
1 tsp (5 ml) baking powder
½ *tsp (3 ml) baking soda*
½ *tsp (3 ml) salt*
2 cups (480 ml) rolled oats
½ *cup (120 ml) chopped nuts*

Cream butter; beat in honey, eggs and vanilla. Combine flour, cinnamon, baking powder, baking soda and salt; mix well. Stir into butter mixture. Stir in oats and nuts. On greased baking sheet shape dough into two 10x3x1-inch logs. Bake at 375°F (190°C) for 12-15 minutes or until lightly browned. Cool 5 minutes; remove to cutting board. Cut each log into ½-inch strips; place strips on cookie sheet. Bake at 300°F (150°C) for 25-30 minutes or until crisp throughout. Cool thoroughly. Yields 3 dozen.

Approximate nutritional analysis per biscotti:
Calories 101, Protein 2 g, Carbohydrates 14 g, Fat 4 g, Cholesterol 17 mg, Sodium 90 mg

GRAHAM CRACKERS

⅓ cup (80 ml) dry milk
½ cup (120 ml) water
2 tbsp (30 ml) vinegar
1 cup (240 ml) brown sugar
½ cup (120 ml) honey
1 cup (240 ml) canola oil
2 tsp (10 ml) vanilla
2 eggs, slightly beaten
6 cups (1.4 l) whole wheat flour
½-1 tsp (3-5 ml) salt
1 tsp (5 ml) soda

Mix the dry milk, water and vinegar together. In a separate bowl mix the next five ingredients together in the order listed. Blend well to keep the oil in emulsion. Combine the two mixtures. Add the flour, salt and baking soda.

Divide the dough into four equal parts. Place each part on a greased and floured cookie sheet. Roll from the center until ⅛ inch thick. Prick with a fork. Bake at 375°F (190°C) for 15 minutes or until light brown. Remove from the oven and cut in squares immediately. Yields 5 dozen.

Approximate nutritional analysis per cracker:
Calories 93, Protein 2 g, Carbohydrates 14 g, Fat 4 g, Cholesterol 6 mg, Sodium 43 mg

APPLESAUCE-KASHA COOKIES

1¾ cups (180 ml) all-purpose flour
1 tsp (5 ml) baking soda
½ tsp (3 ml) baking powder
½ tsp (3 ml) salt
1 tsp (5 ml) cinnamon
¼ tsp (1 ml) cloves
pinch nutmeg
½ cup (120 ml) butter or margarine
¾ cup (180 ml) brown sugar
1 egg
1 cup (240 ml) unsweetened applesauce
½ cup (120 ml) regular rolled oats
½ cup (120 ml) raisins or currants
½ cup (120 ml) kasha, medium granulation, cooked

Sift together flour, baking soda, baking powder, salt and spices; set aside. In large mixing bowl cream butter and brown sugar until light and fluffy, then beat in egg and applesauce. Slowly stir in flour mixture; mix well. Add oats, raisins and kasha. Drop mixture by teaspoonful onto greased baking sheets. Bake at 375°F (190°C) for 10 minutes or until golden brown. Yields 4 dozen.

Approximate nutritional analysis per cookie:
Calories 61, Protein 1 g, Carbohydrates 10 g, Fat 2 g, Cholesterol 9 mg, Sodium 76 mg

RAISIN-OATMEAL COOKIES

2 cups (480 ml) unbleached flour
1 cup (204 ml) turbinado sugar
1 tsp (5 ml) salt
1 tsp (5 ml) baking soda
1 tsp (5 ml) nutmeg
1 tsp (5 ml) cinnamon
2 cups (480 ml) rolled oats
1 cup (240 ml) raisins
6 oz (180 g) carob or chocolate chips, optional
2 eggs
¾ cup (180 ml) canola oil
½ cup (120 ml) skim milk
1 tsp (5 ml) vanilla

In large bowl sift together flour, sugar, salt, baking soda, nutmeg and cinnamon. Stir in oats, raisins and carob chips. In a separate bowl beat eggs and stir in oil, milk and vanilla. Add to dry ingredients and mix well. Drop from tbsp 2 inches apart on lightly greased cookie sheet. Bake at 350°F (180°C) for 13-15 minutes. Yields 4 dozen.

Approximate nutritional analysis per cookie:
Calories 92, Protein 2 g, Carbohydrates 13 g, Fat 4 g, Cholesterol 8 mg, Sodium 75 mg

GINGERBREAD PEOPLE COOKIES

3 cups (720 ml) whole wheat flour
1 tsp (5 ml) non-alum baking soda
2 tsp (10 ml) ground ginger
½ tsp (3 ml) allspice
½ cup (120 ml) butter
½ cup (120 ml) honey
¼ cup (60 ml) black strap molasses
1 egg or egg substitute

Mix flour, baking soda and spices in medium bowl. In large bowl blend butter, honey and molasses together. Beat in egg. Gently mix into dry ingredients thoroughly. Wrap dough in plastic wrap or waxed paper and refrigerate until firm, approximately 1 hour.

Preheat oven to 350°F (180 °C).

Divide dough into four pieces. Roll each piece out on lightly floured surface. Cut into desired shapes and place carefully on oiled or buttered cookie sheet. Bake in middle of oven for 6-10 minutes, depending on size of cookies. Remove from sheet carefully. Yields 2 dozen.

Approximate nutritional analysis per cookie:
Calories 117, Protein 2 g, Carbohydrates 19 g, Fat 2 g, Cholesterol 18 mg, Sodium 97 mg

ALMOND COOKIES

2 tbsp (30 ml) unrefined vegetable oil
2 tbsp (30 ml) honey
½ tsp (3 ml) almond extract
1 tsp (5 ml) vanilla
1 egg, beaten, optional
½ cup (120 ml) rice flour
2 tbsp (30 ml) low-fat soy flour
½ tsp (3 ml) non-alum baking powder

Mix oil, honey, flavorings and egg thoroughly. Combine dry ingredients. Stir dry and liquid ingredients together. Roll dough into ¾-inch-diameter balls. Place on oiled cookie sheet and flatten slightly. Bake at 350°F (180°C) for 8-10 minutes or until cookies begin to brown around edges. Cool before removing. Yields 2 dozen.

Approximate nutritional analysis per cookie:
Calories 32, Protein .7 g, Carbohydrates 4 g, Fat 1 g, Cholesterol 8 mg, Sodium 13 mg

STRAWBERRY TART

CRUST:
¼ cup (60 ml) vegetable shortening
½ tsp (3 ml) salt
¾ cup (180 ml) unbleached flour
¼ cup (60 ml) ice water

FILLING:
3 cups (720 ml) sliced fresh strawberries
3 tbsp (45 ml) granulated sugar
2 cups (480 ml) nonfat, nondairy topping

Mix together the shortening, salt and flour until crumbly. Stir in the water and blend thoroughly. Roll out dough, adding flour as needed to keep from sticking. Place in a 9-inch tart tin and bake in a 350°F (180°C) oven for about 20 minutes or until lightly browned.

Meanwhile mix strawberries with the sugar in a bowl and put aside. When the crust has cooled, spread 1 cup of the nondairy topping over the bottom. Top with the strawberries, reserving a few for decoration. Cover the strawberries with the remaining topping and decorate. Chill for at least 1 hour. Serves 8.

Approximate nutritional analysis per serving:
Calories 165, Protein 2 g, Carbohydrates 16 g, Fat 4 g, Cholesterol 2 mg, Sodium 48 mg

adzuki beans: Small, dried, russet-colored beans with a sweet flavor used in Asian cooking.

amaranth: A broad-leaf plant that produces seeds that can be consumed like grains–as flour, as whole grain or in dry cereal and crackers. Amaranth is higher than most grains in protein and rich in amino acids, lysine and methionine, which are deficient in beans.

Anaheim chile pepper: A mild green or red chile named after the California city. Anaheim peppers are long and thin; they can be purchased fresh, canned or dried.

anasazi beans: Dried, red and white high-protein beans with a sweet flavor.

appaloosa beans: Used in the cooking of the Southwest.

arame: A fibrous sea vegetable. Soak before using.

Arborio rice: A short, fat-grain Italian rice. Its high-starch kernels are perfect for risotto.

arrowroot: A highly digestible thickening agent for sauces and puddings, made from the dried, powdered root of the arrowroot tuber. It requires less cooking than cornstarch, so it is an ideal thickener for sauces that use yogurt. Mix it with a small amount of cold liquid before adding it to sauces or stews.

baba ganouj: A Middle Eastern purée of roasted eggplant, tahini, olive oil, lemon juice and garlic; served with pita bread.

basmati rice: A fragrant rice associated with Indian cuisine. Both brown and white varieties cook more quickly than other rice.

broccoli rabe: A bitter green that is related to the cabbage and turnip families. It can be braised, sauteed or steamed. Also known as rape (rayp), its seeds produce rapeseed oil, marketed under the name canola oil, second only to olive oil in its proportion of monounsaturated fat.

buckwheat: The triangular buckwheat seeds can be ground finely into a flour, as for blini, or eaten as whole hulled kernels, as in kasha. It is high in protein with well-balanced amino acids and is rich in calcium and riboflavin.

bulgur: Wheat grains that have been steamed, dried and crushed. In the Middle East it is the basis for tabouli, a salad of tomato, olive oil, lemon juice, parsley and mint.

carob: Also known as St. John's bread and locust bean, the carob pod contains a sweet pulp that is dried and roasted, then ground into a powder. It is often used as a chocolate substitute.

chipotle chile: Smoked jalapeños.

cilantro: Also known as Chinese parsley, cilantro is a distinctively flavored herb characteristic of Mexican and some Asian cuisines. The seeds of the plant, coriander, are ground and used in curries.

couscous: Refers to the finely cracked wheat or semolina that, steamed, is the basis of the North African dish often containing lamb or chicken with vegetables, chickpeas and raisins.

enoki: Cultivated mushrooms that grow in clumps of long, thin stems with tiny white caps. They are very delicately flavored and crunchy, best served raw or added at the last minute to cooked dishes.

falafel: Middle Eastern deep-fried patties or balls made from ground chickpeas. They are often served with tahini sauce.

galanga: Also known as galangal, this gingerlike underground stem flavors Indonesian and Thai cuisine. With its orange or whitish pulp and reddish skin, galanga is slightly reminiscent, in color and flavor, of saffron.

gluten-free: Flours and food products from which the gluten has been removed. Some individuals have a severe allergy to gluten.

jackfruit: Grown in parts of Africa, Brazil and Southeast Asia, the jackfruit is an oversize relative of the fig. Used in curries when green and in desserts when sweet and ripe.

Japanese eggplant: Looking a bit like a purple zucchini, the Japanese eggplant is a tender, sweet-flesh version of its large relative. Also known as oriental eggplant.

jasmine rice: A highly perfumed, delicate rice from the Orient.

Jerusalem artichoke: A native American tuber that is a member of the sunflower genus, the Jerusalem artichoke is now marketed in the United States as a sunchoke. It can be eaten raw as a sweet and nutty addition to salads or cooked. A source of calcium, magnesium and iron, Jerusalem artichokes are dried and ground into a flour that can be added as a supplement to breads, cakes and cookies.

jicama: An underground tuber. It can be used raw as a sweet, crunchy addition to salads. Cooked, it will remain crunchy. Low in sodium and calories, jicama is a fair source of potassium and vitamin C.

kabocha: A winter squash with a lovely green skin and a pale orange flesh. Typically about 2 to 3 pounds, it must be halved and seeded before cooking and then can be baked or steamed.

kalamata olive: A soft-textured purple-black olive, the kalamata is soaked in a wine-vinegar marinade to give it its distinctive winelike taste.

kamut: A variety of high-protein wheat grown in Montana from a mere 36 kernels brought to that state during the 1940s. The name comes from the ancient Egyptian word for wheat, and the grain is thought to be an ancestor of grains. Kamut flour ground from the grain can be used to bake bread, although its gluten content is lower than that of conventional wheat.

kanten: A setting agent that has stronger properties than gelatin, kanten is derived from dried seaweed. Also known as agar or agar-agar, it is tasteless, thickens at room temperature and comes in flakes, granules or bars. It is almost calorie-free.

kasha: See buckwheat.

kombu: A member of the kelp family, kombu is a greyish black algae. It is sold sun-dried and folded in sheets. It is an especially valuable addition to soup stock.

kudzu: Made from the root of the kuzu vine (and sometimes called kuzo), kudzu powder is used to thicken sauces and glaze fruits. As with arrowroot and cornstarch, dilute kudzu in cold water before adding it to a recipe.

lemon grass: One of the characteristic seasonings of Thai cooking, lemon grass grows in stalks that are often sold dried. Its sour lemon flavor comes from an essential oil, citral, which is also found in lemon peel.

lumpia: This Philippine version of the egg roll is made with a lumpia wrapper or lettuce leaves enclosing a filling of raw or cooked vegetables or meat in various combinations. The wrapper is made from flour or cornstarch, eggs and water.

marrow beans: Round white beans with a distinctive taste.

millet: Millet's popularity among western Europeans peaked during the Middle Ages, but it remains a staple in India and is still grown in China, Egypt, tropical Africa and South America and Ukraine. It has more protein than rice, corn or oats. It can be ground into a flour for puddings or added to wheat flour for breads and cakes.

mirin: A low-alcohol sweet wine made from glutinous rice and used as a sweetener in Japanese cooking.

miso: A fermented soybean paste made, like yogurt, when a cultured mold is injected into a soybean base. It can be brown, golden or red, depending on the other grains added, as well as on the amount of salt or culture added. Aging also influences color, flavor and texture.

niçoise olive: A small, dark, oil-cured olive spiced with the herbs of southern France, usually thyme, lavender and basil or rosemary.

non-alum baking powder: Baking powder made without aluminum salts.

pignolias: Pine nuts, the seeds of the stobe pine, used in Italian and other Mediterranean cooking and baking.

plantain: Referred to as a cooking bananas. Plantains are cooked at different stages of ripening as the skin goes from green to black. They are treated like a starch and have a squashlike flavor.

quinoa: A rediscovered ancient grain, quinoa was a staple of the ancient Incan diet. It contains more protein than any other grain and offers an excellent balance of essential amino acids. It is also higher in unsaturated fats and lower in carbohydrates than most other grains. It can be cooked like rice but takes only 15 minutes.

shiitake: On the average a 3- to 6-inch mushroom with a brown cap. Shiitakes were originally grown exclusively in Japan but are now grown in the United States as well. Most plentiful in spring and autumn.

shoyu: A naturally fermented soy sauce made from soybeans, wheat and salt.

soy flour: Made from defatted ground soybeans, soy flour is an excellent protein supplement when substituted in small amounts for wheat flour in recipes for breads, cakes or other baked goods. It contains from 40 to 60 percent protein. The proteins in soy and wheat complement each other to form a complete vegetable protein.

tabouli: See bulgur.

tahini: A thick paste made of ground sesame seeds commonly used in Middle Eastern dishes like hummus and baba ganouj.

tamari: Originally a by-product of miso production, this soy-based sauce is more commonly a commercial variation on soy sauce.

tempeh: Made from cultured soybeans, tempeh is a low-fat, low-sodium source of protein originally developed in Indonesia.

tofu: Made when soy milk is curdled and then the curds are separated from the whey and pressed. Depending on how much water remains, the tofu will be firm or soft. Firm tofu has a higher proportion of protein, but all tofu is an excellent source of low-fat, low-sodium protein.

tomatillo: Also known as the Mexican green tomato, the tomatillo resembles a small tomato with a thin, papery covering over a shiny green skin. As the basis for salsa, tomatillos can be used raw or cooked; cooking sweetens their flavor which can be quite acidic.

turbinado sugar: Unrefined, or partially refined, light brown sugar.

unsulphured molasses: Pure, unrefined molasses used as a sweetener.

wakame: A Japanese seaweed high in protein and mineral salts.

wasabi: A Japanese horseradish that can be quite fiery. Ground into a paste, it is served with sushi and sashimi. It can be purchased dry and mixed into a paste much like dry mustard.

yellow-eye beans: Small, starchy beans.

yellow finn potato: A firm, waxy, golden potato useful for all cooking.

INDEX

A

A Balanced Breakfast, 17
Almond Cookies, 215
Almost Chinese Hot & Sour Soup, 70
Amaranth Baking Powder Bread, 27
Amaranth Rye Sticks, 43
Anasazi Bean Spread, 51
Antipasto Rice, 108
Appaloosa Beans & Corn, 118
Apple Dumplings, 19
Apple-Raisin Pudding, 208
Applesauce-Kasha Cookies, 213
Artichoke Chicken, 155
Arugula & Tomato Salad, 91
Arugula-Stuffed Chicken Rolls, 152
Asian Rice-Vegetable Salad, 88

B

Baked Dilled Salmon on Rice, 148
Banana Muffins, 30
Barley-Amaranth Waffles, 14
Basmati Rice Pilaf, 99
Bean & Chile Bread, 37
Bean-Vegetable Casserole with Pesto, 185
Beet-Garlic Relish, 193
Berry Breakfast Cake, 26
Berry-Poppy Seed Dressing, 194
Black Bean Chile con Carne, 162
Black Bean Dip with Marjoram, 52
Black Beans & Couscous, 113
Black-Eyed Pea Habañero Dip, 52
Black-Eyed Pea Soup, 67
Blini, 49
Blueberry-Oat Bran Muffins, 29
Blue Corn-Blueberry Muffins, 31
Blue Corn Bread, 26
Breakfast Hash, 19
Broccoli & Mushroom-Stuffed Potatoes, 177
Broccoli & Red Pepper Tortellini, 123
Brown Basmati Rice Salad, 89
Bulgur-Stuffed Squash, 181

Bulgur Wheat "Sausage" Patties, 18
Burgundy Beef Stew, 163
Burgundy "Spaghetti," 136

C

Cannelloni, 138
Carrot-Banana-Honey Wheat Bread, 35
Chicken-Tortilla Soup, 73
Chile Relleño Casserole, 144
Chilled Dilled Carrot Salad, 92
Chunky Gingered Cranberry Sauce, 193
Cold Tomato-Dill Soup, 59
Colusa Corn Muffins, 33
Corn, Jicama & Pineapple Salsa, 189
Cranberry Bread, 24
Cranberry-Honey-Pecan Crunch Pie, 204
Cranberry-Oat Bread, 25
Cranberry Sorbet, 210
Cream of Asparagus Soup, 64
Cream of Squash-Cilantro Soup, 63
Creamy Blueberry Bisque, 58
Creamy Peach Melba Breakfast Bread, 15
Creamy Polenta with Fresh Thyme, 140
Creamy Tomato-Onion Soup, 62
Cucumber-Yogurt Soup, 60
Curried Baked Beans, 111
Curried Garbanzo Beans & Rice, 118
Curried Whole Wheat Couscous Pilaf, 100
Curry Mushroom Soup, 62

D

Dilled Potato Salad, 93
Dolmas, 54
Dried Tomato-Potato Salad, 94
Dutch Double Dill Bread, 38

E

Egg Noodles with Yogurt-Vegetable Sauce, 135
Ensalada de Tomatillo, 93
Exotic-Style Grilled Vegetables, 173

F
Family Gazpacho, 73
French Lentil Soup, 68
French Onion Soup, 72
Fresh Fruit with Chocolate-Mint Sauce, 203
Frozen Raspberry-Yogurt Cream, 209
Fruit Cobbler, 203
Fruit Parfait, 202

G
Garbanzo-Potato Pancakes, 50
Garbanzo Soup, 69
Garnet Yam Soup, 60
Gazpacho, 72
Gingerbread People Cookies, 215
Ginger Turkey Stir-Fry, 158
Gluten-Free Orange Muffins, 29
Gluten-Free Pancakes, 11
Golden Rice Casserole, 97
Golden Tomato-Vegetable Risotto, 105
Graham Crackers, 212
Grape Juice-Sweetened Corn Muffins, 32
Greek Island Chicken, 157
Green Leaf Brown Rice with Garlic Chives, 98
Grilled Ahi with Mango-Peach Salsa, 148
Grilled Chile-Shrimp Salad, 80
Grilled Summer Vegetables, 174

H
Hearty Clam Chowder, 66
Herbed Honey-Lime Sauce, 196
Holiday Dinner Rolls, 42
Homemade Pasta Sauce, 198
Homemade Salsa, 191
Honeyed Rice & Vegetable Stir-Fry, 186
Honeyed Sweet Potato Biscuits, 33
Honey-Oat Biscotti, 211
Honey Wheat Soda Bread, 23

I
Incredible Low-Fat Chicken Pot Pie, 156
Italian Bean & Pasta Salad, 81
Italian Chicken & Rice, 154
Italian Pistachio Pilaf, 97

J
Jasmine Rice Salad, 87
Jicama, Orange & Onion Salad, 90

K
Kabocha-Pumpkin Custard, 207
Kasha Almond Kugel, 104
Kasha & Black Bean Combo, 83
Kasha Varnishkas, 101
Knishes, 102

L
Lamb Chops with Herb-Yogurt Marinade, 163
Lamb Kebabs with Mint, 164
Layered Root Vegetable Stew, 183
Lemony Lentil Soup, 68
Lentil Curry, 119
Lentil Loaf, 120
Linguine with Honey-Sauced Prawns, 130
Low-Fat Hollandaise Sauce, 197

M
Mango-Citrus Sorbet, 209
Maple Syrup Corn Bread, 27
Marinated Green Bean & Red Pepper Salad, 86
Marinated Pasta Salad, 84
Marrow Beans with Rice, 116
Mashed-Potato Boats, 176
Masto-Khiar Raita, 192
Meatless Shepherd's Pie, 143
Mexican Vegetable Sauté, 174
Microwave Stir-Fry with Chicken, 155
Minestrone Soup, 71
Minted Tofu Dip, 53
Minted Vegetable Dip, 53
Mint Sorbet, 210
Mixed Vegetable Slaw, 92
Molasses-Walnut Wheat Bread, 36
Moroccan Chicken Tajine, 154
Moroccan Couscous, 165
Moroccan-Style Salmon, 147

N
Navy Bean Tarragon, 112
New Caesar-Style Salad, 91
North Beach Risotto Saffron, 106

O

Oatmeal-Raisin Muffins, 28
Orange-Hazelnut Muffins, 31
Oriental Rigatoni with Chicken, 123

P

Pacific Chicken, Shrimp & Kiwi Fruit Kebabs, 153
Pasta & Salmon Hot Dish, 133
Pasta e Fagioli with Basil, 129
Pasta e Piselli, 124
Pasta with Chicken, 134
Pea Pod-Spinach Soup, 74
Pears Eleganza, 201
Peas, Pearls & Carrots Medley, 169
Penne Pepper Pasta, 124
Peperonata of Eggplant with Fresh Thyme, 170
Potatoes with Shallot-Garlic-Onion Relish, 175
Potato-Garbanzo Gnocchi, 139
Potato Pancakes, 12
Primavera Pasta Salad, 82
Puréed Butternut Squash, 171
Purple Pudding, 206

Q

Quick Bean Stir-Fry with Rice, 115
Quick Buns, 40
Quick Mango Chutney, 192

R

Raised Multigrain Corn Bread, 39
Raisin-Oatmeal Cookies, 214
Raisin-Rice Pudding, 206
Raisin Scones, 34
Ratatouille-Topped Chicken, 151
Risotto & Vegetables, 107
Roasted Pepper & Yogurt Soup, 57
Rosemary-Lemon Chicken, 152
Rosemary-Vegetable Focaccia Bread, 47

S

Salsa Variations, 190
Salsa with Fresh Cilantro, 189
Sautéed Plantains & Sweet Potatoes, 175
Scalloped Potatoes, 178
Seafood d'Italia, 139

Secret Chicken Dipping Sauce, 196
Seitan Irish Stew, 166
Sesame Chicken Salad, 78
Sesame Chicken with Mango Sweet & Sour Sauce, 150
Sesame Pasta Salad, 89
Shrimp with Honey Cream Sauce & Spinach Pasta, 131
Shrimp Wontons, 47
Smoky Chipotle Pasta, 125
Sour Cream-Apple Pancakes, 11
Southwestern Chicken Caesar Salad, 77
Southwest Tofu Scrambler, 20
Soybean-Lentil-Rice Loaf, 111
Spaghetti Squash, 172
Spaghetti Squash-Stuffed Peppers, 179
Spanish Pasta Roll, 137
Spanish Short Grain, 98
Spiced Beef with Black Beans & Plantains, 161
Spicy Black Bean Soup, 69
Spicy Brown Bread, 23
Spicy Cucumber-Orange Salad, 90
Spring Ginger Salad, 85
Squash & Millet Casserole, 183
Squash-n-Apple Sauté, 172
Stir-Fried Lentils & Beans, 114
Stir-Fried Noodles & Shrimp, 132
Strawberry Soup, 58
Strawberry Tart, 216
Stuffed Peppers, 159
Stuffed Shiitake Mushrooms, 48
Stuffed Squash, 177
Sunny Tortellini, 126
Surprise Breakfast Puffers, 17
Swedish Rye Bread, 40
Sweet & Sour Fish, 149
Sweet Corn Soup, 64
Swiss-Style Oats, 16

T

Tabouli-Stuffed Peppers, 180
Tamarillo Ratatouille, 171
Tempeh Curry, 146
Tempeh Étouffée, 145
Thai Chicken Noodle Salad, 77
Thai Lime, Herb & Honey Glaze, 195

Thai Steak & Rice Salad, 79
Toasted Amaranth Rolls, 43
Toasted Garbanzo Patties, 120
Turkey Meatballs with Lemon Sauce, 160

V
Vegetable & Herb Curry, 184
Vegetable Pasta Primavera, 127
Vegetable Pasta-Yogurt Toss, 128
Vegetables, Rice & Cheese Platter, 182

W
Waffles-n-Fruit, 14
Wheat Berry Porridge, 16
White Bean Purée, 51
Whole Grain Waffles, 12
Whole Wheat Crescent Rolls, 41

Whole Wheat Pizza Crust, 44
Wild Majudra, 99
Wild Rice & Dried Fruit Cereal, 15
Wow! Waffles, 13
Wrangler Steak & Pasta Salad, 78

Y
Yellow-Eye Beans & Squash Stew, 117
Yellow Potato-Leek Soup, 61
Yogurt-Carrot Soup, 65
Yogurt Cheese Parfait, 202
Yogurt Cream Mold with Raspberry Sauce, 205
Yogurt Dijon Salad Dressing, 194
Yogurt Marinade, 195

Z
Zesty Stuffed Pepper Pots, 180